TO
AFRICA
WITH LOVE

Even the *New York Times* took notice. A special ten-coach trainload of Mennonites from Lancaster, Pennsylvania, arrived at the New York pier of the *SS Deutschland* on February 21, 1934. Three of their number were about to embark as missionaries to dark, mysterious Africa.

The 475 wide-eyed well-wishers toured the 700-foot long, five-deck German liner. Then they moved to the Automat on 45th Street for an evening meal and a two-hour service of song, prayer, and meditation. After supper they reassembled on the ship for further sharing and singing.

At 11:20 p.m. the large group reluctantly left the *SS Deutschland* for the pier. John Mosemann, one of the departing trio, cried out enthusiastically from the ship, "Hitherto hath the Lord helped us! Overhead is His banner! We trust Him for the future! What a blessing it is to carry the evangel to the whole world!"

At one minute after midnight, ropes holding the giant vessel to shore slackened. The final refrains of "God Be with You Till We Meet Again" slipped away into the night. The missionaries disappeared into the darkness of the harbor waters and the unknown beyond. The Mennonite safari to Africa for mission had begun.

The special train hurried its Mennonite passengers back to their farms in eastern Pennsylvania. They arrived home just in time for the morning milking.

An unsuccessful attempt to ford a swollen river between the Belengeti and the Ruana in Tanganyika.

John Mosemann, with water canteen and lunch bag dangling from the handlebars of his bicycle, leaves on his first 30-mile safari to Karungu.

MENNONITE SAFARI

David W. Shenk

Herald Press, Scottdale, Pennsylvania

Mennonite Safari

Copyright © 1974 by Herald Press, Scottdale, Pa. 15683
Library of Congress Catalog CardNumber: 73-21150
International Standard Book Number: 0-8361-1733-6
Printed in the United States of America
Designed by Alice B. Shetler

To
Mother

Who gave her life in sharing the gospel with her children and with her friends in America and in Tanzania, and who now awaits the resurrection when she will meet many brothers and sisters who learned to love Christ because she shared Christ.

The author and his brother, Joseph, holding large papaya at the George Smoker home in Bukiroba about 1947.

PREFACE

I grew up in Africa because my parents were Mennonite missionaries in Tanganyika. So as a youngster I observed the drama of a young church beginning to take root for the first time in the history of a society. But I was torn away from my boyhood moorings in Tanganyika to pursue a college education and search for a wife in my parents' native land, America.

A dozen years later I returned to Tanganyika for a brief visit. At the first opportunity I borrowed my father's motorcycle, put my squirming daughter Karen on the gas tank, and set out to find my boyhood home. It is located eighteen miles from the central station to which most of the missionaries retreated as the process of Africanization gained momentum. As I drove along the dirt road, I could have persuaded myself that nothing had changed. Lazy streamlets meandered across the road the same as they had fifteen years before.

I knew the road well. My brothers, sister, and I used to travel it weekly in a gold mine truck to and from the missionary children's school we called "Hill Top School." I spotted the granite rock pile where the monkeys used to chatter, and they were still there continuing the same old gossip sessions. We passed the bend in the road where as a boy I'd give my bike an extra spurt of power because our African buddies had feared that thieves might be crouching behind the roadside bush. Instinctively I gave the throttle an extra twist, just in case.

But the chattering youngster in front of me kept bringing my thoughts back to the present. Lots had happened since I left Africa as a youth. Now I was taking my own child "home" on the motorbike, much like my father used to bring me home on his bike many years before.

And then I saw it. Bumangi my home! My heart skipped a beat. "Karen," I cried, "there it is! That's where I grew up! That's my home!" We drove up the long lane lined with handsome trees which father had planted and we boys had climbed. I had forgotten eucalyptus and jacaranda trees could be so majestic. We rounded the pile of rocks on which my three brothers and sister and I had often played while waiting for the sound of Daddy's motorcycle returning from some evangelistic jaunt in the bushland beyond our hill. And when we'd hear the cycle's put-put in the distance, we'd race down the lane to meet him. We'd all clamber on board and ride home together to meet Mommy and the warm supper she had prepared. Often it was pineapple upside-down cake with milk.

I parked the cycle in front of the neat, whitewashed, mud brick house where we had lived. The yard was full of happy black youngsters running and playing. That too was like home had always been. I had learned Swahili playing with youngsters like these in our front yard. Just then Pastor Jonah appeared at the front door, and I realized Bumangi wasn't really my home anymore. But Pastor Jonah's warm embrace, his words of thanksgiving, and his welcome into his home quickly turned my pang of sorrow into joy. As we sipped tea, he told me of the work of the kingdom in Bumangi land. He told of the nearly thirty congregations he pastored. When I left for America, if I recalled correctly, there had been only four congregations — all pastored by my father.

Then Pastor Jonah took us for a walk. We passed the dispensary, fully managed by well-trained Africans. It was a neat, modern building, much better than the cement stoop of our back porch where mother devoted ceaseless hours in those early years dispensing pills and urging mothers to feed their newborn babies milk rather than thick, choking gruel.

We took a look at the schools — one for elementary and the other for intermediate students. Well-dressed Africans scurried back and forth directing the educational program. In one classroom students were learning the ABC's, in another the Lord's prayer, and in another the values of African socialism. I remembered helping my father measure out some of these buildings back in the years when missionaries took the first hesitant steps toward accepting government-sponsored education.

I turned and faced eastward, taking a long look at the valley below us, a valley which seems to reach out endlessly until it merges with the undulating Serengeti Plain. As far as I could see, most of the houses had shining aluminum roofs. The grass roofs so common in earlier years were vanishing. Several small lakes glistened in the distance. These were artificial lakes which were becoming the rallying points for new villages and agricultural self-help plans. I knew that these villages were borrowing ideas from the mission stations of an earlier generation when schools and medical services became the focus for a community of progress.

"Pastor Jonah," I asked, turning to my gracious host, "how many of those hundreds of homes spread across the plain and nestled around the artificial lakes are Christian homes?"

"Only half of them," he replied. "You see, we still have much work to do."

"Jonah," I responded, "I think I remember as a boy that your home was the first Christian home in all of Bumangi land. Am I right?"

"Yes," he nodded, "you are right. In those days

there were no other Christians in the whole land. Now there are many Christians."

It was time for us to go. I hoisted Karen onto the motorcycle, and after a final handclasp of Christian fellowship, we were gone. But as I drove away, I determined in my heart to share the wonderful story sometime, somehow of mission as observed through the eyes of a missionary's kid.

Biased? Yes, I'm hopelessly biased in favor of mission. I believe that the greatest event in the life of a people is the coming of the gospel. I believe that the greatest happening in the life of a church is the call to mission.

Emotionally involved? Definitely. That's why I wanted to share the story with others as I had experienced it. But I didn't have time, so I tucked the idea into the "sometime" compartment of my mind.

During 1971 a bout of illness forced me into several months of reduced activity. I was delighted when several friends, and the Eastern Mennonite Board of Missions itself, suggested I write the Tanganyika story during that parenthesis in my activity.

I have simply recorded some of the acts of the Holy Spirit in an era now past, hoping the account will provide useful background for those who read it. Although mission methods and cultural circumstances change, the responsibility to share the good news throughout the world is ever with us.

° ° °

Now, for readers who may not be acquainted with Mennonites, a word concerning the context of this book.

The Mennonite Church developed out of the cauldron of sixteenth-century European faith. The place was Zurich, Switzerland — the year, 1525. A number of Christians had been impressed by Zwingli's Reformed preaching. Unlike Zwingli they began to perceive that

Christian commitment was authentic only when the decision to follow Christ was adult and mature. They believed that the symbol of Christian commitment should be adult baptism, and so at prayer one evening, these brethren baptized each other.

Thus in one stroke the Brethren laid the axe to the state church system. Adult baptism became the symbol of freedom of conscience, for it meant that the person himself, and not the state or church authorities, could determine faith. Consequently these Brethren were severely persecuted by both the Protestant and Catholic authorities. Their enemies called them Anabaptists or the Rebaptizers. They called themselves Brethren.

The movement spread quickly northward into Germany and then through the lowlands. In Holland Menno Simons caught the vision and wrote extensively in defense of the Anabaptists. Gradually his name became attached to the movement, and hence the name Mennonites. In England, the Brethren were called Baptists and were the forerunners of the worldwide Baptist churches of today.

The Anabaptists believed that the New Testament was authoritative and applicable. Consequently they refused to participate in warfare, they did not take oaths, they shunned political involvements, they lived simple lives, they practiced brotherhood, and they did not accept a theology of sacramental grace. They evangelized their countrymen vigorously, and thousands died for their Lord rather than compromise their walk of faith.

Because of continued severe persecution, many of the Anabaptists scattered, moving eastward and westward from their original homes. In 1683 the first group came to North America and settled in Germantown, Pennsylvania. Others followed soon.

Perhaps because of persecution, the Anabaptist Mennonites soon lost much of their original evangelical fervor. They became known as "the quiet in the land." However, in North America renewed evangelical concern began to grip the Mennonite Church during the closing decades of the nineteenth century, and certainly during the present century. This renewed vitality was stimulated by the larger resurgence of evangelical faith within North American Protestantism.

As a consequence of this evangelical revival, the Mennonite Board of Missions (General Board) with headquarters at Elkhart, Indiana, was founded in 1882 to serve the mission interests of the Mennonite Church of North America. The early overseas endeavor of this organization included India and Argentina. Many district conferences of the Mennonite Church also developed their own district mission boards.

The story in this book is about the Mennonite mission and church in Tanganyika (Tanzania). [1] The Tanganyika mission began in 1934 under the direction of the district mission board of the Lancaster Conference of eastern Pennsylvania. This board, founded in 1914, is called the Eastern Mennonite Board of Missions and Charities (EMBMC) or for short, Eastern Board. Its current headquarters is at Salunga, Pennsylvania.

After 1934 the work of the EMBMC developed rapidly. Today 600 Mennonites from eastern Pennsylvania and across North America are serving in home and foreign mission with the Eastern Board.

During the last four decades the EMBMC has undertaken work in five additional African countries: Ethiopia (where the Meserete Kristos Church had developed), Somali Democratic Republic, Kenya, Swaziland, and Sudan. The Mennonite Church General Conference Mennonites and Brethren in Christ are busy in other parts of Africa as well: Ghana, Nigeria, Chad, Zaire, Zambia, and Rhodesia. By 1970 total African membership in these churches was about

70,000. North American, European, and even a few Asian Mennonites have served in church-related programs in more than a dozen African countries.

At this writing the membership of the Mennonite Church of Tanzania is about 10,000. These communicants are concentrated in Musoma District, but there are also Mennonite congregations in far-flung urban centers such as Dar es Salaam, Mwanza, and Arusha. In recent years several hundred Mennonites from Tanzania have begun migrating northward into southwestern Kenya, and others have found employment as far away as Nairobi. Currently nearly 200 congregations are active in Tanzania and about thirty in Kenya.

Most Tanzanian Mennonites farm, but others work in industry, government, or one of the professions. Some manage small businesses. Many of these Christians are discovering that economic development is the major new frontier for church concern and involvement. At the same time they maintain a healthy concern for the evangelization of their fellowmen.

The story of mission and church in Tanzania which follows refers frequently to Elam Stauffer and Phebe Yoder. The selection of these missionaries is rather arbitrary. Others have served with equal dedication and fruitfulness, but the service of these evangels spans the years under review as few others do.

This account is written by a white North American Mennonite missionary to Africa. Because of this, it traces the experiences of the missionaries and the sending church. Hopefully, a Tanzanian Mennonite will write a church history soon as seen through African eyes.

Elam and Grace Stauffer deserve a special word of thanks for the many hours of interview and cups of tea they invested in this project. Without them this book would not have been completed. In addition, I was privileged to sit in on interviews conducted by Ron Anchak, who was researching the Tanganyika Mennonite story for his doctoral dissertation.

Eastern Mennonite Board of Missions and Charities funded this project. Board officers cooperated in every conceivable way to make files and secretarial help readily available throughout the research and writing. Mahlon Hess, Janet Kreider, and Nathan Hege reviewed the manuscript critically and editorially. Rhoda Kennel, Naomi Smoker, and Ruth Ann Hartzler kindly helped type the manuscript.

Many people gave personal advice and added bits of pertinent information and interpretation to the story as it unfolded. These include: Charles Bauman, Ira Buckwalter, Raymond Charles, J. Paul Graybill, Paul Kraybill, Ira Landis, Paul Landis, Donald Lauver, Catharine Leatherman, Harold Stauffer, and Rhoda Wenger. I am grateful to all who helped, and I take final responsibility for any shortcomings in the manuscript.

I am especially grateful to my wife, Grace, who encouraged me throughout the project. My parents and my brothers and sister with their spouses who have lived and served in Africa were also most helpful — Clyde and Miriam, Joseph and Edith, John and Lois, Daniel, and Omar and Anna Kathryn Eby. I am also debtor to a multitude of Tanzanian Christians who have lived Christ contagiously: Salmon Sarige, Jona Itine, Lois Mtatiro, Zedekia Kisare, Nashon Nyambok, and many many others.

David W. Shenk

---

1. In 1964 Tanganyika became Tanzania, reflecting the federal merger of Tanganyika and Zanzibar. Since its work is located on the mainland, the church continued to use its original name, Tanganyika Mennonite Church, until 1972 when a Swahili name was adopted, Kanisa la Mennonite, Tanzania (KMT) — Mennonite Church of Tanzania. Hereafter these new names will be used at the appropriate places, particularly in the last chapter.

INTRODUCTION

On the occasion of the fortieth anniversary of the Mennonite Church of Tanzania, their many friends join in greetings of fellowship and in prayers for them. We of Lancaster Mennonite Conference have particular reason to praise God for the blessings that have come to us as together with them we sought to follow Jesus. For our thanksgiving and intercessions David Shenk has provided a launching pad. He has summarized the story and has given some leads in understanding what happened to us through the experience.

This monograph is not a definitive history, but an interpretation of the events. The presentation is not chronological, but thematic. David has sketched for us the themes which emerged as he reviewed the story. History, like life, is all of one piece and the strands are intertwined.

History lovers will welcome the release of Ron Anchak's research findings (mentioned in preface), a professional study of Mennonite efforts in Tanganyika from the beginning through 1960. It will be interesting to discover, which of Shenk's insights are confirmed, and which impressions might be corrected by deeper research into the facts by a person with less emotional ties to the events.

Of course there is still another side to the story, the experiences of the community which hosted the missionary team. On numerous occasions many of us have shared with them in praising God for their entrance into the kingdom of Christ. But someone must also tell, painful as it may be for us, the story of the trauma caused by human shortcomings in the sharing of the gospel. Through the telling we will be saved from glorying overmuch in the small part we had in the planting of a church. Both we and our Tanzanian brethren will have a fuller perception of the grace of God that came to both of us. The telling can minister to the healing and growth of both churches. Let me reiterate David Shenk's invitation to an East African historian to write that story.

Let us recognize, however, that neither Shenk's popular presentation, nor the Anchak history, nor any other undertaken at this early stage can be more than a preliminary study. We do not yet have all the facts, such as quiet ministries behind the scenes and particularly that of prayer helpers. And we do not yet have the verdict of history. We can trace the broad outlines of what happened, but some of the fruits of these vents have not yet ripened. Might some moves which seemed right at the time later be seen to have been less than the best?

While we have only partially perceived all that happened in the planting of a new church, our hearts are full of praise. Our Lord Jesus Christ is building His church! Despite our faltering efforts, what He has begun He will complete!

While redeeming East Africans, our Lord also began saving their overseas guests and partners from sins not before realized. As one brother put it, "What would have happened to our Lancaster Conference if we had refused the discipline of getting involved in overseas mission?" This story too is incomplete.

So let us, Mennonites of North America and Mennonites of Tanzania, make this anniversary an occasion when we open our hearts anew to the grace of God.

Mahlon M. Hess
Eastern Mennonite Board of Missions
and Charities

16

CONTENTS

1. PHEBE'S PROMISE
(Beginning)

Things were topsy-turvy in 1934. For most Americans it was not a happy time. The Depression was five years old with more to come. Thirteen million Americans were out of work. Banks were closing in quick succession like firecrackers on a string. Farmers could not sell their wheat and the price of beef on the hoof had just slipped another penny or two.

A thousand families a day were cashing in their home mortgages in a desperate attempt to find money for bread. It was a time of ferment. The whiff of socialism was in the air. Even the normally apolitical Mennonites were perturbed by Roosevelt's New Deal wheat quotas, and the newly mandated Social Security numbers seemed to some prophetic soothsayers to augur the imminent end of the world.

The Eastern Hemisphere was also edging toward disaster. In the Far East, Japan's war machine had begun chiseling into the Chinese mainland. The Germans had just acquired a new Führer, namely Hitler. In Africa's eastern horn Mussolini's Italian corpsmen were feverishly throwing a ribbon of macadam across Somalia's arid brushlands in preparation for the "Wal Wal incident" of 1935 and the subsequent Italian plunge across Somalia into Ethiopia. Imperceptibly the holocaust of World War II had already begun.

The euphoric dreams of this century's first decade had evaporated — dreams of a world forever subservient to Western Christian culture. Even the churchmen were in a tailspin. Only a generation before, the Edinburgh Missionary Conference had plotted to evangelize the world within twenty-five years. But World War I and then the financial trauma of the Depression had shattered the plan. By 1934 mission retrenchment was more easily contemplated than advance.

The Mennonites of North America had been touched only lightly by the world upheavals during the first third of the century. These pious farmers, commonly known as the plain people, were relatively sheltered and secure. Those of the Lancaster area of eastern Pennsylvania were especially blessed, for they faithfully tilled some of the world's most fertile land. They practiced their faith vigorously and jammed their churches so full for Sunday night revivals that on at least one occasion those responding to the altar call had to walk forward through the crowd on the tops of the benches. The vitality of these revivals doubled Mennonite Church membership in many communities and it propelled the Lancaster area brotherhood into its first mission venture abroad. Although 1934 was hardly an appropriate time to begin mission work in Africa, they did it anyway.

Why did they begin? To probe the beginning of the story, one must turn the clock back to the happier era of 1915 and travel from eastern Pennsylvania 2,000 miles west to an isolated wheat farm on the plains of Kansas. It was there in the heart of twelve-year-old Phebe Yoder that the Lord planted the seed of a vision which the Mennonite Church could not evade.

The quiet drama began simply. At prayer one day Phebe answered a quiet call from the Lord. "Yes, Jesus," she said. "I will go to Africa with You."

No one knew of this commitment, only Phebe Yoder and the Lord, but she never forgot the call or her promise. From that moment Phebe began a venture of faith one hesitates to write about, for it is in a word *sacred*

But you must know, for the history of mission is the story of people, and Phebe is one of the people.

Phebe prepared to go to Africa. She went to Hesston College in her home state and then on to Goshen College and Seminary in Indiana, earning both her BA and ThB degrees. In the process she met a fine Christian man. Their friendship led to love which was Christian and mature, and he asked her to marry him. Then for the first time Phebe shared with another person her agreement with the Lord to go to Africa. But her lover would not go to Africa, and so the engagement never materialized.

After graduation she taught at Hesston College and then in New York City. She prayed constantly for a way to get to Africa. She attended General Mission Board meetings regularly, hoping they might decide to send someone to Africa. But there was no money.

Prompted by the Spirit to additional faith action, Phebe began sending her tithes to the General Board earmarked, "Africa Mission." This accumulating money was a prod of conscience for mission executives. Yet as the years dragged on, the only action taken was talk: We must be realistic, you know. After all, these are depression years!

One day while caring for some children on a crowded New York beach, the Lord shocked her by giving a new command. He said, "Phebe, get nurse's training."

She protested. It seemed so irrational. She was a teacher and doing well in her profession. But there was no escaping the command. So she entered nursing school at La Junta, Colorado.

Halfway through nurse's training, she learned that the Eastern Board, not the General Board, would enter Africa. The General Board's Africa funds were transferred to the Eastern Board. She was heartbroken. "Lord," she cried, "no one in the East knows me. I'll never, never get to Africa." It was a terrific test of faith. In those days one never volunteered. And in those days the Eastern Board was quite exclusive.

As she neared graduation, Phebe received another jolt. The administration asked her to become a nursing instructor. Again she fled to her room and wept before the Lord. What should she do? The answer came, "Wait for three weeks before responding."

About a week later a letter arrived from Orie O. Miller, Eastern Board Secretary. He wrote, "I don't know you, but for nine months have been searching for a nurse, mature in years and Christian experience, to go to Tanganyika as a missionary."

Of course, Phebe went.

But long before Phebe went, the Spirit of God had begun prodding Lancaster area Mennonites to action.

While still a child, Phebe Yoder promised God she would serve Him in Africa. Here, many years later, she is shown teaching a literacy class in Tanganyika.

For thirty some years these Mennonites had been involved in a small home mission program, and they were not adverse to foreign missions. They sent $500 or $1,000 now and then to the General Board for the work in India and South America. But men of vision knew that was not enough. Conference laymen prodded leaders to action. Some were aware of funds for "Africa" accumulating in General Board coffers, and some wished that the Eastern Board could cooperate with the General Board in the evangelization of Africa. Between his Florida winter hibernations, Eastern Board Chairman John Mellinger would slip a foreign mission item into the board agenda time and time again. The widely known and respected Bishop Noah Mack, newly ordained J. Paul Graybill of the Philadelphia mission, and others preached missions. Slowly conscience and vision developed.

Simultaneous with the growth of mission vision, disillusionment with General Board efforts in India swept the Lancaster area. Reports circulated that India Mennonites sometimes wore moustaches, and that the missionaries lived in ostentatious bungalows and identified too closely with the life-style of British colonial authorities. Some of the missionaries, it was said, had discarded their plain clothes.

These reports disturbed Lancaster Mennonites. Mission giving for India slowed to a trickle. A young Sunday school superintendent at Erisman's Church discouraged any further support for the India mission program. This thirty-year-old idealist was Elam W. Stauffer who four years later boarded a ship as the first Mennonite missionary to Africa. [1] His concerned conservatism was typical of the Lancaster brotherhood at that time.

Eastern Board executives were hesitant to launch a new mission in virgin land. They urged their bishops to consider requesting the General Board to administer an Africa venture subject to Lancaster Conference discipline, supported by local finances, and staffed by Lancaster personnel. The administrators feared the legal implications and administrative headaches involved in launching anew. The General Board was experienced, had the necessary connections, and was equipped to sponsor any new foreign mission endeavor which might develop. Vigorous debate continued on this issue for some five years, but finally a decision was made to go it alone.

But where to go?

Abyssinia (Ethiopia) seemed the place.

Why?

Because Mennonites were needed in Abyssinia. Had not the prophets declared that in the last days Ethiopia would reach out her hands to God?

Who should go?

There was lengthy, spirited, prayerful debate on that one. Two couples would form the vanguard. They should be mature. They should be childless and likely to remain childless, for they would need to be rugged frontiersmen in the truest sense. They must be intelligent and healthy. They must be deeply committed to the gospel, and Lancaster discipline, and the "all things." [2] And so it was that Elam and Elizabeth Stauffer and John and Ruth Mosemann were finally selected.

The Mosemanns were sent to New York City to study Bible and tropical medicines. The Stauffers sold their Rhode Island laying hens, Guernsey cows, plow, corn sheller — everything — and left their lovely farm. Elizabeth went to Eastern Mennonite College (EMC), Harrisonburg, Virginia, to study Bible. Elam began a dizzy round of deputation work, telling the constituency about Africa and the witness planned. Professor D.

Ralph Hostetter of EMC told Elam once, after a vigorous question and answer period by a highly inquisitive congregation, "They act as though you have already been there!"

The missionary appointees were heroes to the Mennonites of eastern Pennsylvania. The mood of the brotherhood was euphoric. Meetinghouses were jammed time and again to listen in awe as Elam enthusiastically explained in vivid detail projected plans. It soon became clear that some other Protestant groups in Ethiopia would not welcome the coming of the Mennonites, but that did not dampen enthusiasm. To Africa they would go and, under the leading of the Holy Spirit, a place for mission would be found even though it might not be Ethiopia.

There were several farewells climaxed by a massive meeting at Weaverland. Even today, forty years later, one can hardly find a Lancaster area Mennonite over fifty who does not remember the events of those days with thankfulness. In many homes scrapbooks still adorn mantel shelves or attic boxes with well-thumbed pages holding pictures or clippings of those days.

A nineteen-year-old girl [3] who witnessed the farewell at Erisman, the Stauffers' home church, probably expressed the feelings of thousands in poetic lines:

Well, dear Erismans,
Did you realize what took place yesterday,
When so many people came inside your old doors?
Listen, and I will whisper it to you.
It was a farewell meeting. . . .
When one of our own congregation,
Yes, mind you,
One that came here in his childhood
Gave his farewell sermon,
As he is going as a missionary. . . .
A missionary is one who leaves his homeland. . .

And usually the comforts of a civilized country,
To go and tell heathen and folks who don't know
About God who sent His dear Son into the world,
Lived here and died for them,
That we might go free.

Of course, home ties are strong,
And didn't you see the tears that the folks had to
    shed? . . .
But they are going to Africa,
For that dark, dark continent,
They are leaving tonight.
Therefore, creak ye old doors upon your very
    hinges,
For a foreign missionary is going forth from your
    very doors!
Support them by your prayers, as well as your
    means.
Dedicate yourself to watchfulness and prayerfulness,
And if any more from among your number are
    called to go,
Creak upon your old hinges, and let them go forth,
Till all the world shall shine with the glorious
    gospel.

Grace B. Metzler (Stauffer)
December 6, 1933

Orie O. Miller and Elam Stauffer left in December
to "spy out the land." [4] Only three months later, the
Mosemanns and Mrs. Stauffer sailed for Tanganyika,
which Orie and Elam had selected for the Mennonite
mission in Africa.

Four hundred and seventy-five Mennonites from Lancaster County and the East boarded a special ten-coach
train on February 21, 1934, to accompany the three
new missionaries on their way to New York to embark
for Africa on the *SS Deutschland*. The *New York Times*,
Time Magazine, the Associated Press, and others carried the story in detail.

This train carried 475 enthusiastic Mennonites to New York in February 1933 to see John and Ruth Mosemann and Elizabeth Stauffer embark for faraway Tanganyika.

Arriving early in the afternoon, the party toured the 700-foot long liner which boasted five decks, a crew of 400, and accommodations for 1,200 passengers. Then they moved to the Automat on 45th Street for their evening meal and a two-hour service of song, prayer, and meditation. After supper the group reassembled on board the ship for more prayer, Scripture reading, sharing, and singing songs such as "Love Lifted Me" and "Oh, for a Heart to Praise My God."

Ira D. Landis reported in *Gospel Herald* that "a representative of the steamship line rejoiced that they could bring both our ancestors over and can now take our missionaries back."

At 11:20 p.m. the large group of well-wishers reluctantly left the *SS Deutschland* for the pier.

As a parting testimony John Mosemann enthusiastically cried out, "Hitherto hath the Lord helped us! Overhead is His banner! We trust Him for the future!

What a blessing it is to carry the evangel to the whole world!"

At one minute after midnight, ropes holding the giant vessel to shore slackened. The final refrains of "God Be with You Till We Meet Again" slipped away into the night. And one in every twenty-six of the entire Lancaster area brotherhood waved their first missionaries into the darkness of the harbor waters and the unknown beyond. The Mennonite safari to Africa for mission had begun.

Phebe Yoder was still studying nursing in La Junta, Colorado, 2,000 miles away. Little did she realize how the Lord was answering her prayers that night, for Mennonite mission in Africa was finally underway.

The day would come when at least a tenth of the Lancaster brotherhood would have served in mission for several years or more, and hundreds of other Mennonites across North America would have caught the urgency of this vision, investing years of their lives also serving Christ in Africa.

But in the meantime, the train hurried its Mennonite passengers back to their farms in eastern Pennsylvania. They arrived home just in time for the morning milking.

---

1. Although other Mennonite groups such as the General Conference Mennonites and individual Mennonites were working in Africa long before 1934, Stauffer was the first missionary sent to Africa by the Mennonite Church of North America.

2. This expression is extracted from the Great Commission in which Jesus told His disciples to teach all nations to observe "all things whatsoever I have commanded you" (Mt. 28:20).

3. Twelve years later this same girl went to Tanganyika herself as a missionary. She married Elam Stauffer in Tanganyika in 1949, two years after the death of Elizabeth Stauffer.

4. This expression alludes to Numbers 13:2 when Moses sent twelve men to spy out the land of Canaan prior to Israel's intended invasion.

2.   KATURU HILL
(Settling)

"Lord, don't let them waste a penny of money or a minute of time." The secretary in the London office of the African Inland Mission had intoned his blessing on the two Mennonites en route to Africa in search of a place to start a mission. Orie Miller and Elam Stauffer, the scouting team, had left New York harbor in the closing days of 1933 to spy out the land. They were gathering all the information they could from other mission societies before proceeding on to Africa.

Orie, wearing a long black tie under his neatly fitted plain suit, businesslike, sophisticated, with a quiet, firm faith, believing yet planning, picked up his worn briefcase and walked out of the office. Elam, farmerish, but confident and convinced that what God had begun He surely would complete, closed the door behind them.

Once out in the hallway the younger Elam turned to his senior. "Orie, these mission administrators make me feel rather strange."

The older man nodded sympathetically. "We aren't used to so much praying, are we? They pray when we enter their offices and again when we're ready to leave. Perhaps they realize better than we do that unless Providence is with us, we'll mess things up."

Providence — a factor too often ignored, and never comprehensible. Providence is the kindly, quiet way God goes about arranging schedules, programs, and events for the sake of His children. He never fumbles. Divine guidance is comprehensible — God nudging a person this way and that.

God not only leads the believer, but He prearranges

Friends and relatives stand along the dock as Orie O. Miller and Elam Stauffer sail from New York on December 7, 1933, to seek a mission field in Africa.

events and people to fit into His plan, and accomplishes it without violating the freedom of those involved. This is one of the great mysteries of the Christian way!

Providence found a corner in Tanganyika for Mennonites. Even before Orie Miller and Elam Stauffer embarked from America, the Holy Spirit seemed to be prodding the brotherhood in a gentle, general way toward northeastern Africa. Northeastern Africa is a vast area as large as the United States apart from Alaska.

Other missions had been tilling the soil and planting seed for two generations and more before Mennonites arrived on the scene. It is a rule of Christian courtesy that one does not harvest where others have sown. Thus, the Mennonites needed to find their field in an unworked area.

29

The courtesy principle simplified locating the spot. Wherever they went, Orie and Elam asked mission officials, "Where should we go?" And already in London a location kept popping into conversations: a neglected but heavily populated area on the southeastern shores of Lake Victoria. This area had been avoided by other missions because only small language groups were pocketed there. Most mission societies preferred larger tribes which could be more efficiently evangelized.

European missiologists had also suggested that Elam and Orie consider a totally unevangelized area in the wild swamplands of southern Sudan. So after leaving Europe, the men investigated Sudan briefly. They journeyed southward from Cairo through Egypt to Khartoum, the famous Sahara Desert capital on the Nile. But once in Khartoum they quickly decided that Sudan was not their Macedonia. The reason? There was no railroad into the south, and a quick examination of Orie's datebook made clear that Orie could not afford a fortnight or two churning a thousand miles up the torrid Nile in a river launch looking for places to send missionaries. Checking mission sites by rail was more efficient, and Tanganyika had a railroad. And so with thankfulness for the Lord's nudgings, they embarked for Dar es Salaam, Tanganyika.

Orie and Elam faithfully communicated these signposts from the Lord, step by step along the way. Letters trickled home from Stateroom 492, *SS Bremen*; from Founders Lodge, London, England; then Berlin, Germany; Trieste, Italy; Cairo, Egypt; Khartoum, Sudan; Port Aden, Aden; Zanzibar Island; and finally Dar es Salaam (the haven of peace), Tanganyika. At every stop they were encouraged by fellow Christians with names which sounded rather strange to Mennonite ears: McLeish, Richter, Dawson, Gibson, and Bishop Chambers

The two men pushed on rapidly by sea and land arriving at Dar es Salaam, Tanganyika's coastal capital, only a month after departing from London. Within two months of embarkation from New York, Elam Stauffer stood atop Katuru Hill at Shirati, his future African home. This fast-moving drama of discovery was extraordinary in those days when airplanes were rare, and passable roads often nonexistent.

In Tanganyika the two men had anticipated weeks of inland travel for counseling with responsible mission directors. But God planned better. Just as they arrived in Dar es Salaam, missionaries were convening in the town for the first country-wide conference of Protestant missionaries! And as Orie and Elam shared with these Christians, they knew the Lord had led them well. The other missionaries urged the Mennonites to accept responsibility for evangelizing the half million people pocketed on the southeastern shore of Lake Victoria. The area was known as Musoma District. The British colonial officers agreed enthusiastically. In keeping with colonial law, half-price train tickets were issued for an investigative trip.

Elam and Orie made prompt plans to leave for the interior, and cabled home the good news. They also requested that Elam's wife and the John Mosemanns embark for Tanganyika promptly. Orie accompanied Elam some 700 miles to Mwanza, a lake port at the end of the rail line, where they found African Inland Mission folks who were cordial and helpful. Assured that Elam was in good company, Orie returned to the coast to proceed to India. He never saw the site selected for the mission until eleven years later, when he rode there by car.

Perhaps Orie did not enjoy bicycling, or did not relish eating *ugali*, or feared dhows on rough lakes, or disliked the sting of mosquitoes and the dark wetness of

31

tropical rain on canvas at night. More likely, he had a schedule problem. In any event, Miller, then forty-one, was not to be blamed for entrusting to his younger partner the rugged 25-day exploratory trek through uncharted bushland.

But Elam did not safari alone. Emil Sywulka, a Defenseless Mennonite serving with the African Inland Mission (AIM), accompanied him. Brother Sywulka tirelessly helped the Mennonites find their nook in Musoma District, 150 miles north of Mwanza where he lived. The missionaries felt close to him and called him "brother."

The Africans called him "praying shoes." That was because his dusty black shoes always turned up sharply at the toes. Perceptive Africans knew that only the shoes of a praying man get twisted into that shape. Brother Sywulka loved to pray. He laughed and he cried as he prayed, and God responded. He had been praying that someone would come to share the gospel in Musoma District, where perhaps a dozen small tribes remained unevangelized. At first he seemed surprised that the Lord had sent Mennonites to answer his prayer. But soon Brother Sywulka opened his heart to Elam and did all he could to help him establish a Mennonite mission.

As Elam walked and cycled north across the rolling Tanganyika plateaus with Brother Sywulka those weeks, he sensed that the Mennonites were not the real frontiersmen. Countless others had gone before and the Mennonites would learn much from these other brethren. The Sywulkas themselves had come to Africa at the turn of the century when railroads and highways were nonexistent. Those were difficult years, when missionaries dreaded to get news from another station for fear it would tell of another colleague succumbing to the fever and the call of death. Yet out of these heroic efforts of faith, God had begun to establish a church. By 1934 small churches were emerging even in the areas assigned to the Mennonites.

Elam and Brother Sywulka and their porters pressed steadily northward, clinging closely to Lake Victoria's eastern brim. They traversed 200 miles of swollen rivers, highlands, and swamplands, and not infrequently the muddy track stalled their bicycles. But at last on Wednesday, February 14, 1934, they arrived at Shirati Village, astride Lake Victoria's eastern shore.

They met the local tribal king. He was gracious, hospitable, and eager for a mission to grow in his community. The great man showed them a gently sloping hill, Katuru by name, two miles from the lake, with an extensive view to the north, east, and south. They looked out across a succession of rolling hills, broken occasionally with granite protrusions. Westward from the site stretched Lake Victoria, held aloft by East Africa's massive plateaus. (The lake is 3,700 feet above sea level. It is the source of the Nile River and rivals Lake Superior in size.)

What a site! Gentle lake breezes cooled the weary men. Rhino, zebra, and antelope grazed nearby, stirring Elam's hunting instinct. But Elam was apprehensive about the lack of people in the vicinity. He saw animals in abundance, but the nearest concentration of villages was two miles away. However, Brother Sywulka pointed out that in Africa there is a frontier between animal land and inhabited land. The human frontier keeps moving. The ideal location for a station is just at the edge of the frontier. Then as the frontier moves on, those interested in the gospel will settle near the mission.

Brother Sywulka was right. Today Shirati is an extensive complex with a heavy population scattered throughout the hills and valleys around the center. The

Shirati church is filled with several hundred worshipers every Sunday.

The Mosemanns and Elizabeth arrived as scheduled. Elam met them on the coast. Orie arrived back from India in time to confer with the group and bid them farewell. Shortly the four new missionaries were on their way to Shirati, a thousand miles of weary safari inland by train, truck, and boat — the final lap by lake dhow (a sailboat). Finally the tired couples settled into a native courthouse near the Shirati pier, six miles from the station site on Katuru Hill. It rained the first night; in fact, it poured.

Weeks and months of intense language study, building, and adjustments followed as the four novices began to carve homes and a Mennonite church out of the Shirati bush. Imagine the frustration of learning a strange language with no teacher, while carrying on a full building program at the same time. Imagine the stress of the wives in planning meals with unknown food. Was it spoiled or wasn't it? The flour got wet on the dhow, so what should they do for bread? There were complex logistics of getting cement on site for the building work. Add to the ingredients torrents of rain, flooded rivers, boats that sometimes sailed and other times did not.

Illness was a constant threat on remote Katuru Hill in those days, and struck often. A simple slab of stone under a giant tree marks the first grave on Katuru Hill, that of the Stauffers' stillborn child. Often at sundown Elizabeth would slip out to the graveside and weep alone, unnoticed by anyone, except the Lord. And then Elizabeth became ill. Her heart began to fail, some thought because of the high altitude. Nevertheless, she bravely persisted in her mission, assisting her husband and others, undergirding the work with her prayers, and maintaining a pleasant home until

Elam and Elizabeth Stauffer and John Mosemann share with some of the local people on a Sunday morning in July 1934. Notice the temporary house behind them.

the Lord called her through death in 1947.

Looking through the diaries of these early years, certain words recur again and again: *tired, wet, weary, ill, rain, fever, waiting.* Other kinds of words also sprinkle the entries: *rejoicing, good message, full church, children in church, very encouraging, prayer, letters from home.*

Slowly a station developed. Then other stations were built, too. The plan was to begin five stations, and within six years five had indeed been opened: Shirati, Bukiroba, Mugango, Bumangi, Nyabasi. By 1970 there were seven stations. [1] A station in embryo consisted of a missionary residence, church, and garage. At first all buildings were of mud brick and then whitewashed. Except for corrugated metal on the missionary residences, roofing was of thatched grass. These stations dotted an area approximately the size of Lancaster County, and each served a different language and tribal group.

Other missionaries soon came to help that first little group. Within a year Clinton and Mabel Ferster arrived at Katuru Hill to help in station building, and Dr. Lillie Shenk (later Kaufman) and her nurse assistant, Elma Hershberger, offered their medical skills. In 1936 theologian John Leatherman and his wife, Catharine, arrived followed within months by Clyde and Alta Shenk from the heart of Pennsylvania's farmland. Fulfilling her girlhood dream, Phebe Yoder arrived in 1937. The next year Lancaster businessman Ray Wenger and his wife, Miriam, as well as the Eby Leamans and Dr. and Mrs. Noah Mack joined the growing force of missionaries. Next on the scene were Dr. Merle Eshlemans, teachers Vivian Eby (now Denlinger) and Rhoda Wenger, and evangelists Simeon and Edna Hurst. George and Dorothy Smoker braved wartime travel to come in 1942. They arrived safely, but all their possessions were torpedoed to the bottom of the sea.

With the commissioning of each new evangel, mission interest intensified in another segment of the home church. One ventures that Elam Stauffer was the bishops' man. But with the sending of the Ray Wengers, the Mennonite business community took note, for he was one of them. Clyde Shenk ignited fires of committed interest among the farmers. The Eastern Mennonite College clique were touched by the Leathermans' departure. With Phebe's commissioning, western Mennonites were drawn into the Africa vision. With each farewell, giving would increase as more people felt prodded to involvement.

What kind of people were these missionaries whom the Mennonites sent to Africa?

To this day Africans enjoy discussing these missionaries around their evening campfires, rehearsing some funny and some not-so-funny idiosyncrasies of those white-faced strangers who brought the gospel to their land. Missionaries earned nicknames like Loud Mouth, Humped Back, or Jolly. Fortunately, African courtesy hid these nicknames from the missionary, but if the missionary had begun to assume that he might be one of God's special saints during those farewell experiences in America, he soon knew differently when confronted by the nitty-gritty of Shirati or Bukiroba life.

The missionaries were committed Christians. They had been touched by the Spirit and were driven to share the good news with others in Africa. Their life-style was out of step with that of most white men the Africans knew. While it is true that some Africans remember best the hot temper of one missionary, others remember equally well the day that missionary repented and found victory over his temper. Others tell of the day an African workman accidentally threw a huge blob of mud into the face of a missionary and the missionary laughed! That was Christianity in action, and Africans recognized it as such.

The missionaries were also dedicated Mennonites. The church's examining committees performed their work well, and the team on the field reflected the more conservative concerns of the Mennonite Church. They fellowshiped with other Christians, but refused to be drawn into undue association with such groups. They preferred close communion and at first scheduled their own distinctly Mennonite "spring" and "fall" communion services. They restricted baptism to adults who were evidently Christian, and they excommunicated apparent backsliders. They were concerned about establishing standards of plain dress in the newly forming African congregations. A large triangle of white muslin was adopted as the expected prayer veiling for women converts. One of the major items considered at the first African church council in 1935 was the question of plain clothing in the African culture.

The missionaries were alert. Considering the limited anthropological tools available at that time, they possessed exceptional cultural sensitivity. Yet they were caught in the trappings of that era. A veteran missionary reported that he has never used the word "heathen" in his speech or writings. Yet he did. His articles were peppered with the word. Perhaps the meaning of the word changed in these thirty-five years, perhaps he has changed, but more likely the whole climate of our era has changed.

When Elam landed in Dar es Salaam, he commented that the civilized (European) section of town was beautiful while the African section showed marks of heathenism everywhere. Today we recoil at such statements for several reasons. In the intervening years we have been rudely reminded that Western civilization itself can be most demeaning. The Africans have demonstrated that pre-Christian African culture included aspects of obvious worth. And the awesome economic and educational devlopment of Africa puts its nations on an equal footing with many others around the world.

The missionaries did not bring with them a noxious and impenetrable armor of "knowledge." Their generally unsophisticated academic background did not keep them from learning. Every new sight was an education worth noting. Information was greedily absorbed: "There are seventy-nine horses in all of Tanganyika. . . . There are few animals and many vehicles in Dar es Salaam because the tsetse fly is hard on animals. . . . There are fifty-nine Americans in Tanganyika. . . . It costs $50 to build a nice African hut. The mud walls and high roof make it quite cool. The palm leaves are applied much like we place shingles on American roofs. . . . Some natives have large holes in the earlobes for carrying ornaments, but that is an old custom."

Writing home, Elam described significant experiences such as a funeral procession, African drum beating, foods, dress, and habits. He wrote with intense and sympathetic detail.

But foremost the missionaries were evangels. At every new station a service was held the first Sunday the missionaries were present. The gospel was proclaimed. Even when building work sapped energies and language study hounded waking hours, village visitation was a first priority and the sharing of the good news a daily vocation. God blessed their witness. Within ten years the church had taken root with approximately 200 baptized members participating in a dozen little congregations scattered throughout the region.

The missionaries feared establishing institutions, for they believed these might divert them from the task to which they had been called. They had a clear vision of God's will for their Mennonite Church in Africa. It would be indigenous — self-supporting, self-propagating, and self-governing. But neither missionary nor home church comprehended what those nice words meant.

The missionaries were teachers. Within weeks of arrival at Katuru Hill, they began reading classes so that potential Christians would be able to read God's Word for themselves. Catechism classes were conducted for converts, and within two years the Bukiroba Bible School was already underway. Theologian Leatherman solicited home-church support for the project with assurances that this school would not fall into the secular trappings of other mission training schools. He wrote: "We are organizing a teacher-training school to be conducted along strictly evangelical lines, having as its objective the equipping of native men for an active gospel ministry among their own people."

Throughout these years there was intense involvement with the home brotherhood. At times the newly arrived missionaries felt smothered with letters. Elam wrote that it took him a full day to read the weekly mail. Perhaps some of these letters were too congratulatory. In any event, the missionaries once threatened to refrain from writing home if "we learn or are made to feel that in any way the news we send home is being gathered to make records of accomplishments of people, organizations, or denominations, thus getting the vessel in the foreground and the Master in the background."

Yet the missionaries fueled interest back home with their vivid descriptions of "fierce looking heathen," "difficulties of climate," "feelings of despair," "scorpions with the sting of death," and "muddy safaris." Missionary life was obviously tough and, both at home and on the field, the overriding theme was one of thanksgiving for prayers answered.

---

1 Principal stations and dates of opening are: Shirati (1934), Bukiroba (1935), Mugango (1936), Bumangi (1937), Nyabasi (1940), Kisaka (1954), Migori, Kenya (1969).

3. SPIRITS, WIVES, AND CUSTOM
(Learning)

"It will be different there, you know," highly respected Bishop Noah Mack said as he ushered young Elam Stauffer aside for a moment of quiet talk. "And you should know that the bishops and Mission Board members trust you. That's why we've selected you."

It was late 1933. Bishops and others were impressing Elam with final bits of wisdom before his planned departure for Africa a few weeks later.

Bishop Mack continued, "Polygamy will certainly be one of your major problems. I would not be too surprised if you would find it necessary to admit first generation polygamists into the church. It might be that is what Paul implies when he told Timothy that leaders are to be monogamous."

Elam nodded thoughtfully as the bishop continued, "We in America will not be able to decide these matters for you. But we will pray for you. We believe that the Holy Spirit will guide you well. The African Christians themselves will be your chief counselors."

The bishops knew that they in America could not anticipate the issues confronting an emerging church in Africa. They also knew that the missionaries were foreigners to Africa. It was imperative that Africans themselves find the answers to local issues.

Consequently, as soon as believers were baptized in Tanganyika, church elders were selected and in time, church councils formed. This was the pattern in every congregation. And immediately the African church, along with the missionaries, became involved in the exciting, unpredictable dynamics of seeking Spirit guidance and Bible truth to confront knotty problems. Decisions were reported home, of course. Even though some solutions seemed strange, the home church did not intrude.

Pre-Christian Africans were dynamists, believing that spirits are present in everything. The spirits need to be appeased and manipulated to insure tribal or personal tranquillity. Some people gain special prowess with the spirits and become effective witches, medicine men, or rainmakers. But even the unskilled in the ways of spirits learn to secure themselves by wearing fetishes, avoiding nighttime travel, or planting cactus hedges around villages.

African Christians did not shed their dynamism automatically with Christianization. That should not be hard for Western Christians to understand. We have relics of dynamism hidden away in the recesses of subliminal memory too. The current revival of spiritism is evidence enough, and why the nervous jokes about Friday the thirteenth and black cats even among the most sophisticated?

The missionary novice may assume these forces to be merely superstition, but rarely does the veteran missionary dismiss the spirits lightly, and the traditional African never does. Some Tanganyika Mennonite missionaries remember the time a local rainmaker was beaten for refusing to call for rain. He was flogged until he consented to cooperate, and within a day the rains descended. Bumangi folks tell of the thunderous night the lightning ignited the grass-roofed church house. All Zanaki land knew this to be the work of potent spirits, for only days before several missionaries had inadvertently angered the tribal gods by climbing a hill, Ehazi, where the gods lived amidst a unique cluster of rocks. There are countless stories of deaths and mysterious healings wrought by spirit power.

The great issue in African Christendom is Jesus Power versus spirit power. Yet the dynamism question never appeared on early Mennonite Church council agendas in Tanganyika. This is partly because missionaries couldn't comprehend the spirit world. Interestingly, when Africans talked about spirits with missionaries, it was usually to share how Jesus Power had miraculously delivered them from spirit fear. This kind of deliverance had to be the work of the Holy Spirit. It wasn't a matter you could make rules about. It was rather a thing to be experienced. And in this Africans gave the lead.

In the late thirties Zephania Migire preached a sermon at Shirati which astonished everyone. He declared that spirit fetishes worn on the body were sin. The Christian should trust Christ and not fetishes for protection from spirits. The missionaries did not know that Christians were wearing fetishes! The Africans had not realized that fetishes and Jesus do not go together. The devils were astonished, too, and deeply angered. They set out to get Zephania.

The next Sunday Zephania left home early to preach at a bush church. Fifteen miles down country he and his bicycle collided with a cobra snake. Both cycle and Zephania fell on top of the cobra, with the angry snake thrashing and striking wildly. Slowly Zephania untangled himself from the snake and bicycle. The cobra slithered off into the bush, his nasty mission from Satan accomplished. Zephania surveyed his dirty, bloody, tattered trouser legs, and decided to write a note to his wife before death seized him. But as he wrote, he felt urged to check his bloody leg more carefully. He found that he had not been bitten after all. Although his leg was scratched and bloody there were no snake-bite markings.

With joy he rode on to his destination. What a ser-

A public worship service near Shirati about 1937.

Elam Stauffer baptizing a new Christian in 1935 with Zedekia interpreting. During the last prayer, a large poisonous snake passed between Stauffer and the woman.

44

mon he preached to that little congregation. Even Satan's messenger of death, the cobra snake, had no power over him, he rejoiced, for Christ is Lord indeed. After the message a woman in the congregation shared that she had been warned in a dream the night before that a cobra would attack Zephania on the road to the church. Her husband confirmed his wife's story and said he had had difficulty restraining her desire to do something to help the poor man!

The good news of Christ's victory over the snake traveled throughout the Christian community, and increasingly the gospel was seen as the way to destroy spirit power. Slowly the burning of fetishes became a part of the conversion acts of renunciation of things past. When a pagan [1] burned his fetishes, this was a powerful testimony to his certainty that Jesus Christ is victorious over spirits. Burning fetishes was no joke! It cut deep. And that, too, could not be legislated by councils. It only takes place when people were freed by the Holy Spirit from fear of Satan.

In those early years a Zanaki carpenter at Bumangi, decided to make a bed. He needed some wood and went hunting for appropriate trees. Inadvertently, he began cutting down a tree in a grove sacred to Zanaki women spirit specialists. The women were furious and threatened him with awesome curses if he did not retreat from his act of spirit defiance. He replied that neither he nor the local missionary feared their impotent spirits, and he'd return for the tree to prove to Zanaki land that spirits could not harm people who loved Christ. The gauntlet had been cast, and although the missionary wished he could run from the challenge, there was obviously no alternative except to follow the brave lead of his African brother. They took the tree, and Jona hewed it into the pieces he needed for his bed.

The witches and their cohorts called a conference. They dug a grave to bury those who would die from their curse. Thirty women dressed in lion skins and headgear of wildbeast beards and armed with sticks came to the mission to cast a spell on it and on Jona in particular. Like Israel at Jericho, they circled the mission time after time. The missionaries were afraid, but Jona, the carpenter, assured them that Jesus could not be beaten. The spirits didn't have a chance. And indeed, they didn't! Nothing came of the curse. The good news spread all over Zanaki land. People far and wide learned that the spirits were afraid of Jesus Christ and His people.

In the traumas of frontline battles such as these the Holy Spirit defined the issues of Christian faith versus the spirits. And the gospel message spread that Jesus Christ frees from spirit fear and spirit power. That was good news! Even children understood it. A simple but effective testimony was the straightforward statement: "I used to stay in my hut at night, but now I'm not afraid to venture outside."

While Africans were learning about the power of Christ, missionaries often worried about other things. Some leaders among the new Christians were sporting moustaches. A concerned missionary pastor approached his African colleague concerning the worldliness on his upper lip. "But Pastor," the brother pleaded, "I can't afford a razor. I pull my whiskers out, and pulling whiskers on the upper lip hurts!"

But this is not to imply that the Africans were unconcerned about ostentatious dress and grooming. When long trousers began to appear in Indian shops, African leaders preached with conviction against the worldliness of long trousers. That was a shocker to Mennonites who emphasized the virtue of keeping arms and legs modestly covered. But throw in an African sermon or two on the sinfulness of parting the hair, or the vanity of African women growing long hair, and the missionaries may be forgiven their befuddlement.

However, when Lancaster bishops finally got around to urging plain coats for African men as the most simple solution to the nonconformity issue, the missionaries were unanimous in their opinion that the Africans were well able to handle those issues without externally induced confusion. Distinctive garb has not been an issue in East Africa, probably because both missionaries and Africans quickly found themselves involved in so many other questions that it seemed inappropriate to add that one to their agendas.

But one issue never went away. That was the marriage question. Every church council, every leader, every layman wrestled with it in conscience and in vigorous discussion. Many prayed and wept about it. How can the Christian doctrine of the sanctity of marriage develop in a society where tribal customs and mores do not support that ideal? Marriage issues existed long before Christians came. An estimated 95 percent of the East African court cases were about knotty marriage problems. Throw Christian ideals into that complex, and you have problems disconcerting even to the wisest. Bishops in America recognized this and staunchly resisted any tangles with the marriage question.

In 1936 Elam Stauffer took a trip to Majita land, where a group of believers wanted to be baptized as Mennonites. He was depressed to find that all of them had been married at least twice, and none of them had the remotest chance of returning to the original partner. The bride wealth in this tribe was so small that breaking up a marriage had become an accepted pattern. Child marriage was practiced, and then in adulthood a more substantial marriage arrangement was established with a new partner. To the great consternation of the congregation, Elam refused to baptize these eager converts. He returned to his missionary friends to report that there could never be a Mennonite Church in Majita land, unless it were a church of celibates. But as the missionaries prayed, the Spirit reminded them that salvation is for all people including those in Majita!

Wisely, Elam traveled the 150 miles to Mwanza to discuss the problem with Brother Sywulka and his associates before returning to Majita. This trip reminds one of the Apostle Paul conferring with the Jerusalem brethren to learn whether his gospel was on the mark. [2] The Mwanza brethren confirmed that their Mennonite colleagues were on course. Assured by the Lord that redemptive grace eradicates past sins with the commission, "Go and sin no more," Elam went back to Majita and joyously baptized all who presented themselves. The grass on the roof of that church house quivered as that little congregation filled the building with the strains of "Oh happy day. . . . I am my Lord's and He is mine. . . . 'Tis done, the great transaction's done. . . . Oh happy day. . . . Oh happy day!"

But on the question of polygamy, the church found it more difficult to be redemptive. For a polygamist to send away his wives was usually very difficult to do legally or honorably. Sometimes it was impossible. Yet the believing community feared that accepting first generation polygamists into the fellowship would forever undercut efforts to achieve the Christian ideal of monogamy. This concern was reinforced by the harsh reality that the great temptation of monogamous African Christians was to yield to social pressure and take a second wife. Brethren in the church maintained their Christian ideals at great personal cost. In African culture a second or third wife seemed as right and necessary as an automobile in American society. How could

Christians within the church resist the temptation to take a second wife if polygamists were allowed to become members?

The Mennonites were not alone on this. Except for the Salvation Army, other denominations had taken similar stands. But African and missionary leaders were often criticized for their inflexibility. Some felt the decision was imposed by missionaries, a claim the record does not seem to support. It was rather a position acquired mutually through much prayer and travail. While on the surface the position did not seem redemptive, there were hard realities which the church could not realistically evade. Consequently, the consistent position of the church has been that polygamists should divest themselves of all but one wife, usually the first, before baptism.

But the church hesitated to lay down universal dogmas on marriage problems. Rather each situation was reviewed and a decision sought under the leading of the Holy Spirit. In the case of very old people, there might have been quiet exceptions even on the polygamy question.

Introducing the gospel into a culture is profoundly revolutionary, but especially as it affects marriage relationships. East Africa is no exception. God has created beautiful Christian homes, hundreds of them. Even pagan observers nod their heads in appreciation. The economic realities of modern life plus the continuing infusion of Christian ideals will in time relegate polygamy to the customs of an era past.

The church also struggled with various tribal customs. One tribe knocked out the six lower front teeth as a tribal mark and puberty rite; others made large holes in the earlobes inflicted facial markings, or filed the teeth into arrowsharp points. Most practiced male circumcision and female clitoridectomy. The church struggled with these practices, pointing out to adolscent converts that the body is God's temple and should not be mutilated. Puberty rites often involved pagan ceremonies which were unchristian. Yet community pressures were intense and only a few were able to resist.

The first to break free of tribal shackles usually faced the brunt of battle. Stephano Tingai's wife was the first Christian to refuse tribal rites in Zanaki land. When she became pregnant, her relatives spirited her away to forcefully administer the rites. But Stephano was too quick for them. Running to his wife's village, he manfully intervened. In such situations tribal law dictated that the baby must die at birth, so the Tingai family went to the mission hospital for delivery. Somehow the authorities heard of this, and police compelled all relatives of the family to appear before the district officer before the Tingais returned home. The British officer informed the relatives that if anything happened to the baby, he would discover why, and they would be held responsible. The baby is a lovely, intelligent young lady today, the first living Zanaki whose mother refused to participate in the tribal rites.

That was a generation ago. With more and more Christians penetrating tribal life, mores and values have changed dramatically. Clitoridectomy is frowned upon by educated Africans, and the custom is dying out. The change in attitudes has been so radical that adults frequently go to hospitals now to have tribal markings removed, and only a few young people submit to the former tribal rites.

Unfortunately, older people rarely become Christian. One reason was that Africans usually equated literacy with Christianity. Missionaries frequently made reading a tentative condition for baptism, for they felt that all Christians should be able to read the Bible. Obviously they did not intend this principle to apply to the elderly, but it reinforced the myth that Christianity was the faith of those who could read. Yet miraculously a few very old people caught a glimpse of the light and followed it with all their feeble might. Probably no event in a community spoke as loudly as an old person burning his fetishes. This was irrefutable testimony to freedom from spirit fear. On such an occasion a congregation would spend hours together in joyous song. The Africans realized far more than the missionaries what such a step involved.

At home in America people were glad that churches were being established. Nice letters drifted back and forth across the oceans. Then just before the second world war, Henry Garber, president of the EMBMC, with his wife, Ada, and Bishop Henry Lutz visited the African church. This deputation symbolized the suffering of mission in that they shared the difficulties of travel over bad roads and through arid areas, and that the bishop nearly died from an acute attack of malaria. It also demonstrated the trust of the home church in their mission team by ordaining Elam Stauffer bishop. Three years later Ray Wenger was ordained bishop as well.

It was a happy time, a time for learning new things about Jesus' power, gospel grace, and brotherhood. It was also the pleasant calm before the storm, for in 1942 God shook the Mennonite Church in Tanganyika to its foundations.

---

1. Pagan as used here refers to religious faith which is outside the stream of revelational monotheism.

2. Galatians 2:1-10.

4. FIRE FROM THE HIGHLANDS
(Reviving)

Out of the dreary mountains of little Ruanda. Out of a minuscule kingdom perched astride Africa's Western Rift Valley. Out of the caldron of suffering and failure. Out of the equatorial center of the "dark" continent the little flames of revival began. First they were flickering and fleeting, but then stronger, until a mighty fire spread over eastern Africa.

It reminded people of a handful of brethren in a Zurich prayer meeting who ignited the sixteenth-century Anabaptist conflagration, which all the swords of Europe could not extinguish. Or the time when John Wesley's heart was "strangely warmed" in a small prayer meeting in a room on Aldersgate Street in London. That touch from God stimulated revival fires throughout the entire English-speaking world and had a tremendous impact on early American spiritual and moral life, an impact which in some respects continues to this day.

Jesus told Nicodemus that the Spirit of God works like the wind which blows here and there, yet no one really knows from whence it came or where it is going. Such is revival history, the story of Spirit action, which cannot be captured, contained, or understood. Revival is also like the flickering flame of a newly struck match. God is always starting little fires. He does it whenever a person meets the Lord. But sometimes in God's own way a little flame becomes a conflagration. That is revival.

In East Africa revival began inauspiciously in Ruanda, when a British physician, an African government clerk, and several others began an experiment in transparent fellowship and quick repentance for sins discovered in their lives. Through their experiment they experienced the truth of Matthew 18:20: Whenever believers meet in fellowship, Jesus stands among them. It was as simple as that.

Phebe Yoder had not yet begun nurse's training at La Junta and Elam Stauffer was still collecting Rhode Island Red eggs at noon each day in Lancaster County when the good news of revival began to spill out of Ruanda's hills onto the plateau lands of the Congo to the west and the lakelands to the north, east, and south. The Good News moved slowly eastward around Lake Victoria's northern and southern shores. In 1942 the renewal touched the recently established Mennonite enclave in Musoma District on the lake's southeastern shore.

By that time many of the Mennonites were hungry for revival. Several years before the good news reached them, they had joined with thousands of others throughout East Africa in an intense prayer battle for the touch of God. Everywhere people sensed that something was wrong. They poured out their hearts in evangelistic efforts and Christian instruction, but the power was gone. Excommunications were often 50 percent of baptisms. Some of these excommunications were triggered needlessly and unredemptively. Mission machinery moved rather smoothly, but the gospel was not as effective as Christians believed God wanted it to be.

Missionaries and Africans moved in a climate of fear. Africans feared one missionary's temper and detoured around his house whenever coming on station. Missionaries mistrusted each other because of gossip mills which all seemed powerless to stop. At a Shirati church council meeting in the early 1940s the missionaries were perturbed when the African elders announced that they would refuse to talk about any church problems until the biggest problem of all — wages for church leaders — was resolved. The missionaries laid it on the line, explaining in straightforward terms that such ideas were unscriptural and against indigenous principles. Their support would have to come from the local constituency. The missionaries felt the African brethren were at fault for wasting an entire church council meeting on money matters making it impossible to discuss more pertinent issues. This atmosphere of fear and blame was not conducive to spiritual vigor.

Doubtless prayer cells were the John the Baptists of those years, preparing highways in the hearts of people for the Spirit of God. Since those were the war years, travel and institutional development were drastically restricted and people had time to pray. Four o'clock prayer meetings — a.m., that is, afternoon prayer meetings, evening moments of prayer. Perhaps even more remarkable than the actual outpouring of the Spirit was this urgency to pray which gripped Christians of every denomination and tribe. God's people were getting ready for fresh experiences of the good news.

When the Lord came, His appearance was dignified, purposeful, and powerful. Sister Rebeka Mukura from Mwanza was God's first special messenger. Because of a dream and the encouragement of fellow believers, she accepted the invitation of her friends, Ray and Miriam Wenger and Phebe Yoder, to visit Mugango. At Mugango the Lord revealed to Sister Rebeka that the leading church elder was hiding certain sins. She rebuked him, and he repented publicly. His repentance was the opening wedge of the Spirit in that congregation. The fire of conviction, fueled by her quiet exposition of the Scriptures, swept the church.

Shortly after that on August 8, 1942, two hundred people gathered in Shirati Church at 2:00 p.m. to observe the Lord's Supper. But during prayer together earlier that day, the Spirit had warned Bishop Elam Stauffer and other leaders that there was too much sin in the church to proceed. So at the opening of the service this word from the Lord was shared with the congregation.

When the congregation learned that the Lord refused communion, the fire of God swept through the group. Scores of people spontaneously cried out in anguish repenting of their sins. The noise of weeping filled the building, possibly like the rushing mighty wind at Pentecost. People living close to the church came running to see what was happening. They expected to find a free-for-all fight, but what they saw as they peered through the windows baffled them: a whole congregation weeping before the Lord in repentance!

A pagan woman sitting near the front of the church sprang from her seat and ran from the building crying that they were throwing stones at her, that's how deeply the Spirit was speaking. Eight hours that meeting lasted. As evening came the tears were turned to joy. The entire congregation sang and sang as they participated together in the joy of forgiveness. For days after the breakthrough, nonbelievers avoided coming near the church for fear they would have to confess their sins. The pagans throughout the countryside warned, "God has come down on Katuru Hill."

The Spirit descended at unexpected times and places bringing deep conviction to unrepentant people. It was soon obvious that one could not plan or program His appearance. He descended when He chose and used whom He would. The believers soon learned that one could not capitalize on previous acts of the Spirit; a way needed to be found to continue. They learned that face-to-face challenge, repentance, and seeking the Lord helped to keep one in the way.

Revival among the Mennonites was only three years old when the Lord spoke deeply again through the death of Ray Wenger. In 1938 Ray and Miriam Wenger had left a prosperous business career in the United States to share Christ in Tanganyika. In 1942 young Ray was ordained bishop for the churches in the southern part of Musoma District. Ray engaged in extensive itinerant evangelism and was loved and respected by all. But quietly, unexpectedly the Lord called him from this life on June 9, 1945. It was just an attack of malaria, but that brief illness was Ray's gateway to eternity. As believers throughout the Mennonite congregations participated with Miriam and her three young children in this fellowship of suffering, the Holy Spirit fanned the flames of revival anew.

Through these acts of the Holy Spirit, God's people began to understand more fully how terrible sin is and how great the gift of grace. Time and again tears flowed as repentant sinners were drawn to the Lord. But in the same moment joy and song would pour forth in thanksgiving for the blood of Jesus which makes one clean. Lives were dramatically changed through these acts of God. Throughout East Africa today many church leaders are men who were touched by the Lord during those early years of revival. Countless thousands of laymen were similarly transformed. These believers soon came to be called "balokole" (saved ones).

Along with these acts of the Spirit came a new fellowship. One brother tells of driving into a station compound. The missionary left his house, ran toward the visitor, and embraced him with tears and the

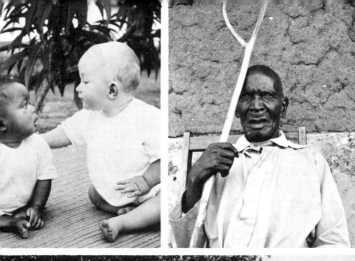

Dorka, an orphan, with Lois Leatherman about 1938.

Elder Ibrahimu from Shirati.

The Mennonite missionaries at Mugango about 1939.

words, "Say, brother, isn't He wonderful!" Prior to this, these two Christians had not been close in spirit, but the Holy Spirit had now created oneness.

This unity found expression in sharing material blessings among believers, but more particularly in spiritual fellowship. However, after four years it was recognized that spiritual vigor had dissipated. A revival team from Bugufi, western Tanganyika, was invited to preach in each church district. Four radiant evangelists, three of them laymen, shared how they had learned to be helped and to help, to repent of sin and to confess it, and to fellowship with the Lord, who stands among believers whenever they meet in His name. Such fellowships sprang up in each area and helped to maintain spiritual vigor long after the first outpouring of the Spirit.

To cultivate scriptural perspective, Bible exploration became a central part of fellowship gatherings. Local groups combined into larger fellowships periodically to learn from the larger brotherhood. Teams of believers circulated among the groups, and thus correctives to isolated excesses or unscriptural tendencies were possible. Occasionally massive meetings were held when several thousand Christians would gather from all over East Africa to meet Christ and one another as a total brotherhood, a practice which continues today.

These fellowships were decidedly transdenominational, but they were usually not schismatic. In a few cases in other denominations fellowship groups were excommunicated. In one such case the believers continued returning to their home church Sunday after Sunday. They quietly stood at the windows to hear the service and handed their offerings through the open windows, even if they were not permitted inside. Their humble persistence won them reentry into their church. Although the "balokole" quickly established a type of spiritual ritual, which included regular fellowship, sin confession, Bible study, and certain song formats, these groups did remain in the established church structure and were a source of creative tension and blessing to the larger bodies.

Interestingly, the revival did not stimulate immediate church growth in Tanganyika. In fact, between 1942 and 1943 the Mennonite Church declined in membership, and several preaching points had to be closed. This was because unrepentant sinners simply left the church. A number of church leaders admitted sin in their lives but, refusing to repent, quit their jobs. Leadership fell apart.

Yet missionaries believed that judgment had to fall on the house of God first, and surely this outpouring of the Holy Spirit was laying a firm foundation for evangelism and growth in the future. They were right. Soon teams of believers began to move out into pagan communities and shared God's Word with power. A new leadership emerged that had been tested by fire, and these men and women became the lively stones the Lord used to build His church.

One is tempted to compare these African believers with the Anabaptists of the sixteenth century. The church as a fellowship of believers was central to both. Both resisted schismatic tendencies. The Anabaptists were not able to overcome the prejudices of the established churches and consequently suffered excommunication, whereas the African brethren did stay within the establishment. Both were intensely concerned with holiness of life, and this piety was expressed in tangibles, such as simplicity of dress. Both were anchored to the Scriptures, although in both movements there were spiritualistic tendencies. Both movements were skeptical of politics and government.

Both insisted on adult commitment to Christ, although baptism as a symbol of that commitment has never been an issue in East Africa.

As the movements aged, both had to cope with the problems of legalized forms, while discovering that detailed codes can lead to internal schism. At this writing the East African brotherhood is coping with modern dating practices. Dating was not part of East African culture and traditionally the revival brethren had not permitted their children to date. But modern Africans feel this should become a matter for individual conscience. Such issues could become schismatic, much like the ban issue which led to the Amish schism in Anabaptism. [1]

Interestingly, probably no Mennonite African took the pacifist position in World War II. Those who were inducted served in the armed forces. This was most disheartening to the missionaries who taught pacifism and had negotiated conscientious objector status with British colonial authorities for African Mennonites. Nevertheless, it is a hard reality that indigenous conviction on nonresistance developed only after the revival, and then it was brethren from other denominations who really showed the way.

When the Mau Mau revolution spilled out of Kenya's highlands in the 1950s, Kenyan brethren refused to join sides. They lived nonresistance at great personal cost, and hundreds, perhaps thousands, were killed by the Mau Mau for their refusal to take up arms, and their positive love actions, such as sharing water or food with all who were in need, regardless of which side they supported. Many officials were convinced that it was the nonresistance of these brethren that eventually broke the back of the hostilities and laid the foundation for a harmonious transition to independence in Kenya.

One is prodded toward the conviction that it was these acts of God which introduced an Anabaptist quality of faith commitment into African culture, rather than any efforts by the Mennonites. However, Mennonite missionary leadership was probably more receptive to the revival than any other group. Their Anabaptist orientation led them to feel quite at home with revival brethren. This leadership commitment to the revival meant that Mennonite African laity were spared the denominational persecution which most other revival groups experienced. However, probably because persecution perfects faith, suffering brethren from other denominational groups have always been in the vanguard of revival leadership. Mennonites have been the followers.

The Holy Spirit constantly prods people off their particular dead center. Thus in the more undisciplined churches, the revival tightened people up. In highly disciplined groups, the revival seemed to loosen things up. The formerly careless felt that he must now *do* something to demonstrate the reality of his newfound pearl. The one who had already been *doing* felt great release in realizing that his works would not get him to heaven, only God's grace would do that.

As mentioned earlier the Mennonite missionaries tended to be rigid. Revival loosened them up considerably. Outwardly nothing changed. Hemlines still clung to the foot-below-knee-level principle. But inwardly they experienced a new freedom which included release from denominational rigidities.

This change in perspectives finally filtered through in letters home. At first the mission board chairman, Henry Garber, urged that all should give thanks for the great outpouring of God's Spirit in East Africa. Later he confessed great concern and some confusion on what the missionaries were talking about. Perhaps he was referring to statements such as, "Mennonitism can't save you, only Christ does that." He agreed, but why were the missionaries so vigorous in stating the obvious? Could it be that they intended to leave the Mennonite Church? Unfortunately transatlantic transportation was paralyzed by the war, and no one could go from America to gain a firsthand understanding of what had happened. When a deputation finally did get to Tanganyika five years after the revival had begun, they were able to say, "What you folks in Africa say frightens us, but what you are doing makes us glad!"

A fresh touch from the Lord is often like a happy wedding. The bridal pair imagine they are the only ones in history who have experienced such joy. People newly awakened spiritually frequently feel the same way. There is quality about each person's encounter with the Lord which is personal, unique, and fresh. God has a special blessing for each of His people. But problems result when the newly born begin to feel that the spiritual experience of others is inadequate or inferior, or that all must have an identical encounter with God.

On the other hand, a Christian whose encounters with the Lord have been quite mundane may be utterly bewildered by the vocabulary and the evident joy of the newly touched. He may feel that the revived brother is fanatically misled, or downright untruthful. He might be jealous. All revivals bring such tensions. And while the Spirit's work in East Africa brought great blessing to thousands, and laid a firm foundation for later church growth, it is equally true that it brought tensions.

As suggested earlier, mission correspondence to the home board frequently triggered confusion. Only months after revival began, a considerable group of missionaries requested that their regular allowances cease. They wanted to live by faith alone. Doubtlessly they wanted to empathize and identify more closely with African church leaders whose congregational support was often rather sporadic. They did not want to enjoy a fixed, guaranteed allowance, while the African leadership lived in the uncertainty of occasional congregational gifts.

Although initially bewildered by the faith leap of the missionaries, the mission board did cooperate. For many years a number of missionaries paid their transatlantic fare, medical expenses, everything, only with funds especially designated by contributors in the home church for their respective support accounts. So far as I know, not one ever went hungry.

A more shattering bombshell fell in 1943. The home office was busily recruiting three or four missionary couples for the Tanganyika Mission. Several people on furlough were preparing to return. Then a letter came from the field secretary stating that no new recruits or furloughed missionaries should come to Tanganyika who were not Spirit filled, or who did not know what the "cross-life" meant. He added that these necessary qualities had nothing to do with adherence to Mennonite discipline, or to the doctrinal questionnaire which all missionaries had to complete satisfactorily. This was the unanimous decision of the field conference body!

The mission board went into a tailspin, but the unruffled bishops advised patience. The home officers did the only thing possible. They stopped processing prospective missionaries and wrote to Tanganyika saying that they respected the field's wish, but that the home board didn't know how to measure the required qualities. Furthermore, the home church did not want to do anything which would disrupt the evident good fellowship on the field. Consequently, no new missionaries would be sent unless the missionaries could give workable guidelines.

The Africa missionaries were chagrined and embarrassed. Before long an understanding with the board was reached and the processing of the new recruits shifted into gear again. Yet this incident was but a prelude to a twenty-year drama wherein home leadership and the Tanganyika Church struggled, sometimes futilely, to find common ground. It was not only the missionaries whose perspectives shifted during traumas of church building and revival. The Eastern Board constituency too was shifting, but the shift in Pennsylvania was toward increased conservatism and doctrinal rigidity. The elasticity of Christian love was severely tested at times under the tremendous pressure of divergent views on fundamental issues. But the elastic never snapped; in fact, bonds of brotherhood grew stronger through the test.

American Mennonites were at least vaguely aware that something rather strange was afoot in Tanganyika. They gleaned this from the circle letters which missionaries circulated to friends and church publications. Three years after the onset of the revival, missionaries began coming home, and few could deny that they seemed to have a more "grace" centered message than earlier. The reaction of many was indifference. Others were vaguely uncomfortable and perhaps even hostile. They feared these missionaries did not have a solid Mennonite emphasis. For many others the good news shared by the missionaries was accepted as a stepping-stone in their own spiritual growth and they received it gladly.

However, for a few American Mennonites the good news from Africa was more than just a stepping-stone. It was the dawn of a new day. I was visiting in Pastor Glenn Zeager's cozy home in Bronx, New York, when he told me what the good news had done for him.

"Tell me about it, Glenn," I invited.

Glenn leaned forward in his living-room chair and looked intently into my face. He began slowly. "I hate to think where I'd be now if it hadn't been for those African missionaries," he began. "I was a chicken farmer in Lancaster, Pennsylvania. My wife was a pretty good Christian, but I couldn't care less."

Just then Glenn's wife, Florence, entered, nodding her agreement. "That's right," she volunteered. "Sometimes Glenn did take me to prayer meeting, but he'd sit out in the car and sleep while I'd go inside to pray. It always made me feel so dumb."

"Our home was in bad shape," Glenn continued. "I don't mean that we were going to get divorced or anything like that, but it wasn't good harmony, you know."

He paused to throw a wink at his pert little wife who had now taken a seat opposite his. "Then one day I heard one of these missionaries telling about the love of Jesus and about revival in Africa. I got interested, and then the light dawned. Jesus filled my soul, brother, and it's been different ever since."

After a moment's hesitation Glenn continued, his Bronx drawl betraying the fact that he wasn't a Pennsylvanian anymore. "Shortly after the Lord touched us, we sold the farm and moved to the city. I figured I couldn't tell the gospel to chickens, so we moved to where the people are."

We chuckled lightly, and then the conversation slipped naturally into another vein. "Glenn, tell me about Phebe."

"Oh, Phebe," he responded brightly. "Why Phebe is living right here in our home now. Almost every day she goes over to Fox Street and walks up and down those alleys and tells the people about Jesus. The kids just love her. They call her grandma. Phebe loves it here in the Bronx, and of course we love Phebe too."

As I listened to Glenn, it all seemed so incredible. This was the same Phebe who had promised to go to Africa in 1915 when she was but a twelve-year-old Kansas farm girl. The same Phebe who prayed Mennonites and herself into Africa more than forty years ago. The same Phebe whose Mugango home in Tanganyika was the place God chose to begin His work of revival among the Mennonites in 1942. Phebe had finally retired from her African sojourn in 1971 and she had joined Glenn and Florence to help them share the good news in the seamy alleys of the Bronx.

Certainly had it not been for that fire from God which began spilling out of Ruanda some forty years before, Glenn, Florence, and Phebe would never have teamed together for kingdom work in New York City. And whenever East African revival leaders come to the United States on preaching missions, they stop with the Zeagers for fellowship. Thus the revival which began in Africa's heartland has reached New York City's inner-city morass.

---

1. The Amish schism in Anabaptism developed in Europe during the eighteenth century over the issue of the ban. The Amish believe that one should not so much as eat with backsliders.

5. ASPIRIN AND THE THREE "R's"
(Serving)

"In Cairo I saw pyramids which are thousands of years old. In Bengasi I saw guns which can throw bullets as far as a man can walk in a day. In Rome I saw airplanes which fly as fast as a man's voice. In Marseilles I saw buildings as high as Katuru Hill. And in all the cities I visited, the cars never cease to fill the streets. Their motors are like the sound of a thousand drums."

Five-year-old Man O Wari quivered with pride as he listened to his father — so handsome, elegant, wise, and regal-looking. Appropriately, the man was wearing heavy black army boots, a huge brown woolen soldier overcoat, and a drooping cap accented by a little red feather clinging precariously to its left side.

The embers of the evening's cooking fire silhouetted the faces of eager listeners who crowded near to hear of far-off lands which Man O Wari's father had visited while soldiering for the English. Man O Wari was born when his father was sailing the Mediterranean in a British man-of-war. That's why he was named Man O Wari. Now at last Berlin had been blitzed, Hiroshima lay in ashes, and the gallant soldier had come home to Tanganyika to tell of his adventures.

The soldier continued, almost solemnly. "We must never permit the bloodthirstiness of Europe to seize us. We must cultivate the good that we have, like a farmer caring for his maize."

The listening sages grunted their assent.

"But we must also know that we have much to learn." The soldier's voice was firm and strong.

"We must learn to read and write. We must know adding and subtracting. We must know the story of Jesus, because there is power in that Man. We must understand science. We must go to school."

The soldier's final words were spoken with command. A light breeze caught the words from his lips, and tossed them, as it were, across the land.

The old men nodded in agreement.

The middle-aged nodded too, and so did the youth.

And little Man O Wari shook all over, because suddenly he was terribly excited. He would go to school someday, and he would learn and learn and learn.

And suddenly all of Africa, from the Sahara to Good Hope, from Cape Verde to Cape Guardafui, everywhere a cry went up: "We want schools." And little Man O Wari and thousands and millions like him came crying: "We want schools!" And across Africa the Christian missions heard the cry, and the governments heard the cry, and they built schools. And the Mennonites did their little bit also to help Man O Wari and his friends find a school.

For the first dozen years of Mennonite mission in Tanganyika, educational and medical development were slow. The reason was mutual. Both the Africans and the missionaries feared too much emphasis on building institutions. African sages knew that mission education, and perhaps medicine too, could turn their cozy world upside-down. They did not want that. Missionaries knew that excessive social service would cut into their preaching time, and they did not want that. Then the great war and revival changed everyone's perspective. This is the story of how it happened.

For the early Mennonite missionaries in Africa, Roland Allen's book, *Missionary Principles*, was as authoritative as Daniel Kauffman's *Doctrines of the Bible* was for a generation of Mennonite leadership in

Suddenly, all over Africa, people wanted schools for their children. Mennonites did their bit to help.

America. Allen wrote prolifically during the early part of this century, emphasizing that churches everywhere must be self-supporting, self-propagating, and self-governing. These three rules were biblical. They had an apostolic ring to them. They could all be wrapped up into one concept, namely, indigenous church building.

The missionaries were convinced, conscientious disciples of Roland Allen. Allen's indigenous motif guided their financial policies. Never would they permit money to flow from the United States into the pockets of African leaders. All resources for church extension and nurture had to emerge locally. The only possible exception would be funding for capital expansion such as church buildings, and even that kind of assistance was often resisted.

Allen's principles strongly influenced the missionaries to resist institutional entanglements. There was a two-fold rationale for this. First, institutions were costly to build and operate. They would consume American Mennonite money. That was against the indigenous principle and, therefore, not scriptural. Second, institutions smacked of the social gospel. The task of the church and the missionaries was to preach the gospel of Christ. They would not permit themselves to fall into the trap of misguided priorities. Since they could not do everything, they would largely limit their involvement to proclaiming the gospel.

However, within days of that first missionary bivouac on Katuru Hill, Shirati, some people began pressing for a literacy class. And the missionaries gave in. Obviously potential believers should know how to read the Bible, and believers certainly should. Thus a literacy class was not seen as incompatible with the indigenous principle. Later, as a matter of procedure, a school was opened with each new station, and usually a missionary was given full-time responsibility to teach in the school.

But these early schools were sleepy exercises. Only four grades were offered, and often the classes were only half full. In some communities missionaries scoured the countryside urging children to come to school. Sometimes all they acquired for their efforts were hoots and laughter. At one of these stations, under prodding from the government, tribal leaders actually paid children to attend school in an effort to improve enrollment. And school was considered entirely inappropriate for girls. After all, women could bear children, cook, and carry loads without knowing the alphabet. In most African communities recognition of the bene-

John Leatherman chairs a meeting of the general church council at the Mugango Church in 1938.

fits of formal education developed slowly.

A further problem arose when Africans graduated from fourth grade and became teachers themselves in outlying bush schools, or even in the central station schools. These teachers needed wages. Missionaries urged them to be satisfied with the tithes which the small Christian community offered to the Lord in the weekly worship services. But that wasn't workable. Christians were few and not all of them tithed. In any event, the weekly tithe for a wage earner came to about a nickel a week. Even in 1940 a fourth-grade graduate felt he deserved a more adequate and systematic wage plan.

The impasse was resolved by charging fees to students, but then enrollments dropped. Some schools closed down completely. The idea of paying for education was too far out for most Africans in the early forties.

In 1935 the first medical doctor, Lillie (Shenk) Kaufman, arrived at Shirati. She came primarily to take care of the missionaries, and the missionaries were thankful. But obviously, she could not resist helping Africans who crowded her door for treatment. Thus the mission was dragged almost against its will into an expanding medical program. Progress toward adequate medical facilities often resembled the forward movement of a balky donkey. Repeatedly missionaries warned of the dangers of drifting away from the fundamental task of proclaiming the gospel. They found it hard to fit indigenous principles into a money-consuming medical program.

But the doctors (by 1939 there were two of them) saw things from a different perspective. They were convinced that the gospel includes a healing ministry for the body. They argued that it is unchristian to send professional persons to care for the missionaries only. The Africans too were children of God and deserved just as much professional care in time of illness as the missionaries did. Furthermore, they felt it totally unjustified to invest years of effort and thousands of dollars in tooling up for missionary medical work in Africa, only to discover that the mission's intent was to limit the doctor's activities to handing out aspirin tablets!

For a decade the discussions went on, vigorously at times. In spite of limited facilities, the doctors did their best, and were deeply appreciated by the thousands who came to them.

The great turning point for the Tanganyika mission

came in 1947. That year a significantly deeper spirit of fellowship grew out of renewed revival. Consequently, African leaders and missionaries had an unprecedented conference to determine common goals in education, particularly whether to receive government subsidy and open new schools. They agreed that they had a responsibility, particularly to the children of believers. It was also the year for the first deputation from home in nine years' time, although Orie Miller had made a quick postwar stop in 1945.

The American deputees were astonished to find that their Tanganyika missionaries were ready, and quite eager, to plunge into a full-blown institutional program. Excitedly they showed the deputees their plan. Miller was amazed at the profound shift in their thinking. He pressed them for a rationale, and they had a good one. There was little inconsistency, they insisted, between how they had felt previously and the present decision.

In the first place, immediately after the war tremendous pressures developed from constituency and government for the mission to plunge into education. The war had awakened Africa. Soldiers returning home told astonishing tales about European cities, technology, and chaos. Africa suddenly wanted to learn what it was all about. Now Africans were clamoring to get into school by the thousands, and they implored the missionaries to do everything possible to provide the opportunity. The government launched a ten-year educational plan which aimed to put half the children into primary schools by 1956. The Mennonites had to get into the act, or bow out completely and let the Catholics take the field.

The beauty of the scheme was that indigenous principles would not be violated. These schools would be funded largely from government monies — solid Tanganyika currency. The hitch was that the mission would need to provide certain matching funds for plant expansion and for building and operational costs. However, the missionaries reasoned they would not budget for this needed American money. Instead they would pray about it and send an occasional letter home and to the church papers. Such an approach would not particularly violate indigenous principles.

As for medical facilities, they handed that hot potato to the home board. They reasoned that a larger medical program would be fine if freewill budget funds were provided strictly on home board initiative as an unsolicited gift to the Africans. After all, if God sends you money that you didn't ask for, can it really be all that wrong to use it?

But Orie Miller was troubled. He pointed out that the church was still small with only 313 members. Surely this vigorous institutional expansion would snow the church under. Somehow, he felt, institutional growth needed to be tied to church development. He spoke from the perspective of one who had witnessed too many churches around the world which had been stifled by massive service institutions.

It must be emphasized that the missionaries had not come to this decision quickly, but through prayer and much inner struggle. But for most missionaries revival had taken the edge of fear out of the new. They had a new sensitivity to the aspirations of the Africans. They felt that it was the Lord's will to begin more vigorous educational and medical efforts. To do otherwise would be a betrayal of the African brethren. And they were certain that the Lord Himself would keep the institutions in perspective. So the old fears were quieted.

At the same time they told Orie that their Gideon's fleece would be the availability of unbudgeted funds from the United States to meet the mission's obligations in matching funds. If the Lord did not prod the home constituency to give to these projects, the programs obviously could not continue, and expansion would be out of the question. They would move forward in faith, and accept the Lord's "no" in the form of curtailed gifts from home.

And Orie was satisfied. The education committee was promptly enlarged. Five Africans served with the three missionaries. A new journey had begun.

A year later the schools almost collapsed. Money was not coming from home. Missionaries and Africans joined in prayer. They asked the Lord to show them anything about the educational efforts which might be displeasing Him. Imagine their joy when a large gift came from a home congregation, and the school year ended with all accounts in the clear.

Those were the first timid beginnings but, like a snowball rolling down a hill, the program grew faster than expected. By 1951 they needed to build the first district boys' boarding school, which was for classes five and six. They located it at Bumangi in the cool interior hills. Each Mennonite congregation contributed labor to construct the various buildings. All workers provided their own food. People from Shirati and Nyabasi, seventy-five miles distant, came by truck. Those from Bukiroba and Mugango, each only eighteen miles away, came by foot. The travelers sang Christian songs of praise as they journeyed. One could hear their jubilant songs rising and falling over the Bumangi hillsides long before the tired processions arrived. By the hundreds they came, and how they did work! Station secretary Clyde Shenk wrote home that he had never seen buildings erected so rapidly. A dining hall, dormitories, classrooms, and teachers' houses were all completed in a matter of weeks. Obviously the

Mennonites had struck a responsive chord in deciding to expand their educational program.

Pressure for further expansion accelerated rapidly. Even girls wanted to go to school. Everyone was clamoring for more education. By 1955 missions all over Tanganyika were driven to the wall financially by the tremendous educational development. Neither the Mennonites nor other mission groups in Tanganyika had sufficient matching funds for this kind of prolific growth. So the government provided funding for new schools and the mission administered them. The Mennonites alone needed to develop sixteen new schools in 1955-56 to stay abreast of constituency pressure and to complete what they had undertaken as their contribution to the ten-year plan.

Frantically education secretary Mahlon Hess set about putting prospective teachers into training schools and ordering building materials for the sixteen new schools! It was an incredible exercise, but by 1956 the nation had overshot their goal, and the foundation had been prepared for more steady, sane expansion in the second decade of development.

At the same time, medical program expansion burgeoned also. The doctors were caught up in a whirlwind of healing that involved far more than aspirin. Surgeon Lester Eshleman arrived in 1951 to broaden the mission's medical services. Under the leadership of Dr. Merle Eshleman a hospital slowly spread across the mission compound at Shirati. Several health clinics were built in the hinterland. The era of limiting medicine mostly to quinine, cough syrup, worm medicine, and aspirin was past.

It must be stressed that the church maintained some caution during those years of rapid institutional expansion. Orie Miller, especially, kept a foot on the brake. Many missionaries felt his caution was wise, for they were concerned lest the schools and hospitals eclipse the church. There were others who felt the missionaries were too cautious, notably J. Paul Graybill. Once when education secretary Hess was enjoying a furlough, bishop-educationist Graybill definitely encouraged the secretary to move into secondary education, and the sooner the better. Secretary Hess was reluctant. He was exhausted. There were not enough MA degrees in the Mennonite Church to spare for an African secondary school. But through Graybill's prayers and local demands for higher education, Hess's African educational network soon included an interdenominational secondary school at Musoma.

In 1960 the Tanganyika church became an autonomous conference. That was thirteen years after the 1947 plunge into deeper service involvement.

In those short years institutional development had been phenomenal. By 1960 a fine 100-bed hospital, a 40-student nursing school, and a 300-patient leprosarium were in operation at Shirati. The church had three sizable clinics in remote areas. Four thousand boys and girls were enrolled in the churches' twenty-six registered primary schools. The Bumangi District School, mentioned earlier, had long since become a full-fledged middle school for grades five to eight. The church now operated three such middle schools. One of these was a fine girls' boarding facility, Morembe School, overlooking Mara Bay near Bukiroba station. Nearly 600 students crowded the Alliance Secondary School at Musoma. The Bukiroba Bible School had grown to 20 students. The church employed seventy qualified teachers in its educational program.

In addition there were scattered unregistered bush schools here and there sponsored by untrained but dedicated Christians who wanted to do their part in bringing literacy and faith to the remotest villages.

A printing press at Bukiroba was turning out thousands of printed pages monthly, and there was a bookstore in Musoma.

Of course, by 1970 the various programs had evolved even further. For example, the Musoma Alliance Secondary School had become a six-year school with its upper grades achieving junior college status. The Shirati hospital had been rebuilt with an infusion of German Evangelical Central Agency funds, and a new leprosy control center also graced the Shirati compound. The leprosarium had been funded by the American Leprosy Mission.

In most of these capital projects there was a minimal infusion of Mennonite money, except, of course, for the cost of personnel. Additionally, people within the church were involving themselves in agricultural development projects here and there. Through Mennonite Economic Development Associates (MEDA) American brethren had provided thousands of dollars in loan funds to prospective African businessmen to help them develop viable economic enterprises.

No one in that 1947 special conference could have foreseen where their timid step toward institutional entanglements would lead. In effect, the Mennonites cooperated with government and other agencies in establishing a national system of public education and health services with strong religious orientation! The educational involvement was strikingly parallel to church-government cooperation in forming the American public school systems during the first hundred years of its colonial and national history. Like early Americans, most Africans have had at least some exposure to Christian faith. Many are committed believers.

Best of all, church growth kept pace with educational expansion. Who would debate the rightness of that!

6. THE FISH POOL
(Growing)

The pastor was obviously excited. So were the other members of his family. It was baptism Sunday! They were up by the first rooster crow preparing an African style feast of goat steak and *ugali* for their anticipated guests.

By eight o'clock people began arriving at the church. Some came by bus, others by cycle. But mostly they came walking along winding footpaths. Mothers with sleeping babies cradled on their backs. Young fathers holding the hands of little boys and girls as they walked along. Hobbling old men and grandmothers whose bodies were twisted by age. Students with neatly pressed uniforms of khaki and blue. Some came from over the hill, only a mile away. But others had trekked ten miles or more.

By nine o'clock the neat little church, with whitewashed walls broken at regular intervals by attractively arched window openings, was full. The building boasted a newly installed corrugated tin roof with a little bell perched on top. It was an ancient dinner bell which a kind Pennsylvania farmer had donated for his brothers in Africa. The front half of the church floor was cemented, but the back part was still earthen because the congregation hadn't found the money to finish the floor. The seats were sun-dried bricks, each about nine inches square and twelve inches long. Nearly one hundred brick seats were arranged in random rows.

Half an hour before starting time, each of the seats had an occupant, and some had two. But the people still kept flowing toward the church until the windows and doors were also full of peering faces. At 9:30 the bell on top the roof clanged the audience to stillness and the service began. The pastor and elders led the service with dignity. Two songs, an Old Testament Scripture reading, one song, the New Testament Scripture reading, the Apostles' Creed, another song, and then a fiery sermon about eternal judgment and the love of Christ.

Finally the time for baptism arrived. But the church was too full for the two score candidates to move to the front, and people beyond the door could not see. So the congregation moved outside to the eucalyptus trees along the road. There among the trees the pastor, his assistants, and the candidates arranged themselves for the solemn ceremony. About a dozen were teenage youngsters, first generation Christians. The rest were adults, one a tottery old man nearly blind with age. The crowd stood in a huge, eager circle about the candidates.

After hearing their vows, the pastor called for the water. An elder brought a huge basin full to the brim. The pastor called out loudly as he administered three handfuls of water per candidate, "In the name of the Father, and of the Son, and of the Holy Spirit." The words ricocheted off the nearby granite protrusions. Passersby stopped to take it in. The herdboys nearby stole silently away from their charges to peer between the legs of the spectators or climb convenient trees to observe the man of God baptizing people into the Christian church. Secretly they vowed that they too would be baptized someday.

After pouring the water on each candidate in turn, the pastor and elders moved among the rows of newly baptized Christians, giving them Christian greetings and welcoming them into the Christian church. Then the pastor raised his voice in song. The whole congregation there among the trees joined him in a mighty chorus, "Happy day, happy day!" And then the service was over. Those who had come from a distance stayed to eat goat and *ugali* with the pastor. The rest hurried away for lunch at home.

That night as the pastor knelt by his bed for evening prayers, his heart was thankful for the joys of the day. But as he prayed, a great darkness seized him. Suddenly he knew that he would fail. He knew that he could never adequately pastor those he had baptized that day. They were too widely scattered. The pull of the world would be too hard for many to resist. Their pagan families would do all they could to discourage the new believers. Some, he knew, might never enter a church again, and some would be lost. His job was too big. He knelt there depressed.

Then the Lord came near and spoke, "I, the Lord, will finish the work I have begun in the hearts of those who were baptized today. All I ask is that you be faithful."

"Thank You, Lord," the pastor sighed. And with a free heart he retired in peace.

It was not only the pastor who had qualms about big baptisms Tanganyika style. American Mennonites became concerned about it too.

On a Sunday evening in June 1968 a man and his wife and six children — the Martins, we'll call them — motored east along Lancaster's new beltway to join two or three thousand other mission-interested Mennonites for an evening of inspiration at the big tent on the Lancaster Mennonite High School campus. By 1968 these meetings in the tent at the school had become a kind of late spring ritual for Lancaster area Mennonites. The messages at the tent were a catharsis. Those who came heard how God was using Mennonite cash and people to help the poor and save the lost. That was good for one's soul. The tent was also where you met your friends, and that was a pleasure.

On this particular June evening a missionary bishop on furlough from Tanganyika was to preach. The bishop was known in the American and African brotherhood for his clever way of saying things and his warm Christian concern. By the time Brother Martin had parked his tan Chevrolet at the lower end of the school's baseball field, the tent was already overflowing, so the Martin family stood outside with several hundred others. It was a pleasant evening. The teenagers in the Martin family drifted toward pockets of friends who were also standing outside.

The singing was tremendous — inside. But outside it was overpowered by the solo voice of the song leader booming through the speaker system. But Brother Martin on the outside sang lustily anyway. He especially enjoyed the verse, "Throw out the lifeline across the dark wave. There is a brother whom someone should save." Then the bishop was introduced and he launched into a ringing account of church growth in Tanganyika.

"If present trends continue," the bishop observed "within twenty years there will be more Mennonites in Africa than there are in America. In Tanganyika alone we are baptizing nearly 1,000 people a year. The church is growing 20 percent a year."

Brother Martin shuffled uneasily. Subliminally something bothered him. *How*, he wondered, *can a thousand Tanganyikans a year become good Mennonites?* "Listen to that," he whispered, nudging his wife.

The bishop continued. "The fields are ripe for harvesting. If we don't drive the combines through the fields now, the grain will spoil. Jesus said we are to

82

Sunday morning worshipers following a service at the Shirati Mennonite Church.

be fishers of men, but catching fish with hooks is too slow; we must use nets and bring to shore all that we can. In Tanganyika we accept all who come. We turn none away. The words of the Lord as recorded in the Revelation had become our motto: "Whosoever will may come."

That certainly wasn't the way Brother Martin was used to hearing it said. He knew that the gospel is for everyone, but in his home congregation the motto seemed to be: "We accept only the holy; we turn all others away." That's why the bishop's message made Brother Martin uneasy.

Brother Martin and the pastor in Africa weren't the only Mennonites bewildered by swollen church membership rolls in Tanganyika. During the early Anabaptist period, Mennonites experienced explosive church growth, but seldom since. Rapid growth tends to surprise and even perplex Mennonites.

In Tanganyika the Mennonites were surprised. About 1947 a growth spurt began which propelled thousands of people into the Mennonite fold.

How did it happen?

We can never fully know the dynamics of God's efforts to bring men to Himself. In Tanganyika the growth of educational involvement paralleled the fantastic church growth. One could suggest that the schools siphoned people into the church. But during the first decade of growth, the majority of baptisms were of mature adults who had not been directly touched by the schools. Thus it seems more likely that the first fifteen years of gospel proclamation in Tanganyika had prepared the soil for a bountiful harvest. Revival created a foundation for solid growth. And then the gates of resistance suddenly burst open, and people marched into the church.

This spiritual ingathering coincided with a general awakening to modern life throughout Africa. People everywhere suddenly wanted to leap into the twentieth century. In the process many discovered the church. The church was caught up in the same societal dynamics as schools and hospitals. If the church had neglected the educational aspirations or the medical needs of these marching societies, certainly people would have believed that the church was repressive, reactionary, and opposed to progress. This would have been the ultimate tragedy, and certainly people would have turned from the church in disgust.

When most African nations acquired independence during the 1960s, 80 percent of educational enterprise south of the Sahara was in Christian hands. In almost every area of development, the church was in the vanguard. Consequently Africans on the whole still tend to view Christian faith as the foundation of progress. This is in striking contrast to common feelings about pre-Christian faiths which many believe to be stagnant.

It is right that the gospel stimulates progress. Jesus said as much: "Seek first his kingdom and his righteousness, and all these things shall be yours as well." How fortunate it is that the church remained true to her mission in Africa! The early Mennonite caution about educational and medical entanglements was an appropriate reminder that the bread of life is from above, but slowly the church learned to share material bread by identifying with the legitimate aspirations of a people pressing toward a new future. By identifying with these people, the church was able to share the good news of Jesus in ways which would have been impossible otherwise.

As noted earlier, for the first decade the churches grew very slowly. The first baptismal service was held at Shirati in 1935. Only fifteen were baptized, and six received by letter. After ten years of vigorous evangelism, there were only 163 members in all five congregations. The second oldest station, Bukiroba, had only three members at that time. But only three years later, in 1947, membership had nearly doubled and stood at 313, with 205 additional believers preparing for baptism.

This growth is partly attributable to revival teams who began to move through the countryside sharing God's good news. Also there was a marked increase in growth in the Mugango area following Ray Wenger's death in 1945. He was deeply loved, and the message of his death seemed to result in a new turning to the Lord in the communities he had served. Thirty-one were baptized at Mugango that year.

During the first decade of increasing institutional involvement (1947-57) membership increased from 313 to 1,212. A decade later membership had increased an additional 5,000 and was approaching the 7,000-member mark. Between 1947 and 1967 membership had increased more than twentyfold.

The American brotherhood was probably gratified by this harvest, but certainly did not become euphoric about it. To the home constituency discipleship has always been more important than church growth. They were quite glad to hear of a 20 percent annual membership increase, but quickly the question would pop into conversation: What is the quality of their faith? Some American Mennonites emphasize holy living so much they do not get upset if growth is imperceptible or even if there is a loss in membership. A few even idealize no-growth, observing that it is in static situations that distinctive Mennonite tradition is most purely preserved. Mennonite missionaries have never been pressured to produce spectacular growth. The only mandate has been: Preach the gospel and be faithful.

Doubtlessly this ideal of a pure church contributed to slow growth during the first decade or so of Mennonite mission in Tanganyika. Converts to Christianity were put on a two-year probation before they were accepted for baptism. Even so, excommunications were common. This strategy for church development might be called the fishbowl approach. Only carefully selected goldfish are placed in the fishbowl. Off-color fish are discarded. Growth is not permitted to compromise purity.

However, the revival spoiled the missionaries' fishbowl. During the revival the Holy Spirit showed that no congregation is pure. He shone a spotlight into the fishbowl which revealed the true colors of the fish. All of them were speckled by sin. The Holy Spirit dealt mostly with people who were already members of the church. The revival had little direct influence on pagan communities.

After the revival, fish pool missiology began to replace that of the fishbowl approach. Fish poolers point to Pentecost where 3,000 were baptized in a single day. They suggest that the criterion for baptism at Pentecost was belief in Jesus Christ. The discipling followed that first spark of faith, and careful teaching, as when Ananias and Sapphira died for telling a lie. [1] Hence the argument runs that in a non-Christian community which is turning Christward, all should be baptized who confess that Jesus is Lord and Savior, without worrying too much about the quality of faith. Then these baptized thousands become God's fish pool, where they can be fed and nurtured into the kind of fish God wants. If one neglects enlarging the fish pool, it is suggested, many will be trapped in other pools such as Islam and be lost to the church forever.

This shift in strategy was subtle and never absolute. The ultimate in fish pool missiology would indicate that whole families should be baptized including children and babies. Many denominations did this, but never the Mennonites who always insisted on individual conversion as a prerequisite for baptism. Furthermore, the Mennonites in Tanganyika always maintained a healthy degree of Anabaptist concern for church purity. However, after the revival they were more willing to accept the necessary risks to purity which rapid church growth brings. Probably because of latent purity concerns and resistance to infant baptism, the Mennonite Church was content to baptize only thousands, while many other Christian communities were baptizing tens of thousands.

Rapid membership growth did not necessarily imply larger congregations. Rather, congregations spread throughout the countryside. Scores of laymen heard the call from the Lord to leave the pleasant enclaves of mission compounds and begin new preaching points in population centers here and there.

Typically the church would hear of an area where there was some interest in the gospel. Brethren would pray to the Lord to send forth an evangel. When a family heard the call, the church would help them move, perhaps assisting in setting up the new household. If the evangel could teach, he might collect a bit of money from students who gathered in the small grass-thatched church for daily reading lessons, but his chief livelihood was his garden patch. In the afternoons he walked among the villages sharing the gospel. Slowly a congregation formed. By 1960 there were eighty such preaching points. By 1973 the number of congregations had doubled with 215 preaching centers.

The good news of the revival prodded this sort of mission effort. Through these acts of the Spirit, Christianity was authenticated in African culture. Before revival, most African Christians believed Christianity was the white man's religion. He joined the club to partake of the white man's magic, which included the ability to read and the right to receive injections when ill. But the revival pierced hearts with the message that Christ is for every individual whether African or American. The revival fellowships were a brilliant adaptation of African primary group relationships to the Christian concept of brotherhood and fellowship. These fellowships were an authentically African response to an amazing breakthrough of the Holy Spirit. Thus, congregational extension became a concern of African brethren themselves. It wasn't just the white man's idea any more.

As churches grew, nurture became enormously important. In 1947 under the guidance of George Smoker

Daniel Opanga, longtime composer and pressman at Musoma Press (managed for many years by George Smoker).

the Musoma Press began to print a steady stream of Christian literature on an old-fashioned, inky, small "job" press requiring sheet by sheet hand-feeding. Its little David Bradley power unit faltered too often, but it printed. Thousands and millions of pages of gospel poured out of this antiquated, but sturdy, machine. Typesetting was done by hand. The first major publication was a Swahili songbook called *Tenzi Za Rohoni (Songs of the Spirit)*. This booklet quickly gained an international market. Tracts, Christian nurture materials, bulletins, and booklets were published. Probably the best-known publication was a modest monthly paper called *Mjumbe wa Kristo (Messenger of Christ)*. Thousands throughout East Africa learned to love this magazine with its hard-hitting inspirational articles.

Missionaries and Africans struggled to produce Christian nurture materials. They succeeded in creating an established religious education curriculum for public and church schools in Tanganyika. That was an interchurch project. Denominations also cooperated in creating Sunday school lessons. Sometimes curriculum was painstakingly mimeographed on hand-operated duplicators. Catharine Leatherman, Dorothy Smoker, Alta Shenk, and others invested thousands of hours in writing, producing, and grading these Christian education helps. Mennonites also printed a catechism for baptismal candidates.

Growing churches also needed leaders and in 1950 the first four African pastors were ordained. Other ordinations followed, and African church leadership became more authentically African.

More must be said on these first ordinations. The church was called to prayer and heart searching and Bible conferences in preparation for the selection and ordination. The African churches moved with a sense of awe and expectancy toward the ordination day. A visiting American brother commented to several African leaders that this would be a heavy work. The Africans responded, "Yes, but it is also a good work."

Leaders decided that they would not use the lot; it reminded them too much of pagan magic. Instead, they would pray until the Lord revealed His choice through the unanimous vote of the congregations. People everywhere were urged not to talk about the matter with one another, but rather to pray that God would reveal His will.

In September 1950 people from the whole Mugango-Majita area met to discover the Lord's will. One missionary groaned as he saw scores of illiterate women coming to the meeting. Surely they would not know how to discern the Lord's will. Probably others doubted too. Certainly to expect people from a dozen far-flung congregations to know the Lord's mind stretched faith. Many were immature Christians.

Finally the moment arrived to vote. One by one the Christians filed out to present their votes. An hour later the missionary bishop returned to the audience to call for one sister to return to the anteroom. They privately informed her that all votes fell for two brethren, but she had named a third. Did she feel quite certain that the Lord had led her to cast that vote? She wept, requesting that her nominee be removed. She had named her congregational leader, the only one she knew.

There was no formal closing to that meeting. When the congregation was informed of what the Lord had done, they knelt in thanksgiving prayer and then poured from the doors, singing and raising their hands in worship and joy. Testimonies of praise poured from hearts bursting with thanksgiving.

One veteran missionary says he is still moved as he remembers the joyous songs of the women as they went about their cooking for the worshipers that evening. The beauty of the sunset, the rising choruses from testimony groups gathered here and there, and the singing women as they cooked the evening meal were a wonderful climax to a steep climb in his pilgrimage of faith.

The ordination was held a month later on October 6, 1950, in connection with a previously scheduled Christian life conference. A makeshift grass-thatched flat roof was constructed at the remote little church of Nyamulibwa in Majita. Hundreds came from great distances to witness this first ordination. And what a happy day it was when the Tanganyika Mennonite brotherhood received its first two pastors, Ezekiel Kaneja Muganda and Andrea Mawawa Mabeba.

One month later the Shirati Christians met to choose two pastors. Six names were submitted, and the group was called to further prayer. After another month there was unanimity and Zedekia Marwa Kisare (who is now bishop) and Nashon K. Nyambok were ordained.

That was a generation ago. As the church became more unwieldy, the Africans developed other means of determining the Lord's leading in ordinations. Nowadays ministers are frequently selected by the ordained leadership. A minister may oversee as many as twenty congregations. His duties are much like those of a bishop in the American brotherhood. Elders and deacons assist him in his work. But even these patterns are fluid, for God's church is a growing, changing organism and leadership patterns must be flexible too.

A maturing, growing church should never be trapped in the shackles of obsolete strategies. Consequently, in 1958 the American and Tanganyikan Mennonites began to plan a new partner relationship.

However, before partnership could be effected, serious hurdles needed to be crossed.

---

1. Acts 2:42 and 5:1-11. The biblical record states that after this event great fear fell on the church.

7. BROTHERLY TUG OF WAR
(Disagreeing)

"I'll step on board with you for a minute," volunteered Bishop Elam Stauffer of the Tanganyika Mennonite Church.

"Fine. Let's talk in my state-room," responded Bishop J. Paul Graybill of East Earl, Pennsylvania, who was concluding a fortnight's visit among the Tanganyika Mennonites.

The taller Graybill led the way as the two spiritual sages walked across the gangplank leading from Musoma pier onto the lower deck of a lake steamer, probably the *Usoga*. Both men were in their early fifties, with black hair only mildly streaked with gray. Once on board, they wended their way gingerly past piles of rope and then up a narrow metal stairs to the first-class passenger deck where Graybill had reserved a state-room.

The deck overlooked the pier below, where a swarm of energetic men were stacking goods which the ship had brought to Musoma from ports along the lake, and indirectly from around the world as well — textiles from Bombay, sugar from Kisumu, crates of gold-mining machinery from Edinburgh. Other workers were filling nets at the near edge of the pier with products which Musoma District offered for sale elsewhere.

The day's export was mostly sisal fiber for binder twine for American hay bales. Eager cranes angled above nets spread along the shipside. As soon as a net was filled with bales of white sisal, hooks would swoop down and, after pausing briefly to secure the net, they would heave the precious cargo upward and then inward toward the center of the ship, where the cranes would drop the load into the holds of the vessel. The sisal would be shipped north to Kisumu, sent from there by freight train a thousand miles east to the coastal port of Mombasa, then shipped through two seas and two oceans to America. Some of the sisal fibers on Musoma pier that day have found their way into the very barns of the farmers who filled Bishop Graybill's churches in East Earl on Sundays.

It was a fascinating scene, but neither bishop noticed the drama of prosperous postwar world economics unfolding on Musoma pier on that Sunday morning of June 29, 1952. As they stepped into the state-room and pulled the door shut behind them, each breathed his own private prayer that God would direct their speech.

As they took seats opposite each other, Bishop Graybill came to the point quickly. "Elam," he began, his earnest voice hardly more than a whisper, "the American Mennonite brotherhood is the father of the Tanganyika brotherhood. So the church in Musoma District should accept the paternal concern and authority of the Lancaster Mennonite Conference until the parental church decides to give independence to the younger church."

Elam cut in almost abruptly. "No, Paul. That should not be. The American fellowship and the Tanganyika church are equal in Christ. Therefore the relationship between the two fellowships must be fraternal rather than paternal."

The conversation continued vigorously until the ship's bass whistle warned the two bishops that the time had come to bid farewell. It was a sad parting that day. With heavy hearts the two men of God waved a final good-bye as the boat pulled away from shore.

Slowly the white ship moved farther and farther from the small cluster of African and missionary brethren who stood with Elam on Musoma pier until their brother from America, standing on the first-class passenger deck, faded from sight.

The Stauffer-Graybill parting of 1952 was but a minor incident in the total panorama of relationship happenings which unfolded during the postwar era, but it did symbolize an ideological parting of the ways between the American and African brotherhoods, which but for the constraining grace of God would have been disastrous.

The division between Tanganyika and home church leadership cut deeper than polarization on administrative viewpoints, though, as important and insoluble as these appeared to be. The real problem was trust. When Orie Miller parted with the first little team of missionaries at Dar es Salaam airport on April 6, 1934, he said, "Trust is the only way. We just must trust each other." Tragically, trust was fractured during the 1940s and it took two decades and more to fully recover it.

Both missionaries and home church leadership felt frustrated. On the one hand, the missionaries believed that the bishops at home wanted to pull the rug from under the self-governing leg of the indigenous church. They felt it was unjust to reverse the self-governing processes which the missionaries had begun to introduce as early as 1935 when the first congregational council was created. They believed that the home church should not undercut the right to local decision-making, when the Tanganyika church was so nobly carrying its own financial responsibilities. And most disconcerting was a suspicion that the home church intended to undo the liberty of revival and the authenticity of African Christian experience by pressing the Tanganyika church into Lancaster Conference molds.

On the other hand, the homeland bishops were afraid that the missionaries were trying to "get away with something." Also the bishops feared that any exception in Africa to homeland practice would jeopardize the peace of the American brotherhood. In addition, there was some suspicion that the missionaries might join another denomination, an idea the missionaries always insisted was groundless, but a suspicion which nevertheless persisted.

Probably this clash in viewpoints was unavoidable. From the beginning the mission enterprise was doomed to ensnarement on the horns of a dilemma. The first missionaries had been commissioned to do two things: (1) establish Mennonite churches which would faithfully follow the "all things" as understood and practiced by Lancaster Conference and (2) establish indigenous churches reflecting biblical perspectives in African culture. Those two mandates were irreconcilable, but because of travel inconveniences during World War II, the day of reckoning was postponed until 1947. By then the church had become a teenager. Like teenagers everywhere, it was anticipating adulthood, not regression to childhood and dependency.

These incompatibilities in mission strategy needed to be resolved just as the Mennonites of eastern Pennsylvania, who had been predominantly rural, began the painful transition to becoming highly urban. City life frightened Mennonites, for the city appeared to be a strangling force which threatened to erase Mennonitism from the earth. Consequently, the greater the threat from urbanization, the more important it seemed to maintain a distincitve Mennonite dress pattern. Distinctive dress was visible evidence that the Mennonite community continued to exist even as urban sprawl and its modern paganism engulfed Mennonite homes and communities throughout eastern Pennsylvania. The distinction of "plainness" was often maintained at considerable personal cost, for alien American culture pressed and squeezed the Mennonite community relentlessly.

In those days of crisis people sought for leadership and firm guidelines. In postwar Lancaster County, bishops provided that leadership. Many of them ruled with firmness and authority. The laying on of hands acquired nearly sacramental force and increasingly authority drifted away from the congregations into the hands of the bishops. These leaders carried the burden of church administration with firmness and sincerity. They believed that if they failed, the faith of the fathers would be lost forever. Increasingly, change was equated with drift toward the world. Consequently, they could debate for hours seemingly harmless trivia. But the debate was consistent with their concerns, for the question always posed was: What will this lead to? And in the minds of the bishops, and a majority of laity, that was no idle question.

This growing phobia about change set the stage for a twenty-year debate with the Tanganyika church. Although in the 1930s the scales had tipped in favor of an indigenous church in Africa, by 1947 when the first postwar deputation arrived in Tanganyika, the bishops were not sure that they wanted an indigenous church after all. To them the word "indigenous" opened a Pandora's box of trouble. They were sure that any decision by the Tanganyika brotherhood to depart significantly from Lancaster Conference tradition would undermine stability at home. Furthermore, the Eastern Board planned for new missions in Ethiopia and Central America, with more to follow later. Tanganyika would be the model for church development in other countries.

Deacon Paulo Chai bids Orie O. Miller farewell at the Musoma airport about 1948.

As related earlier, Orie Miller was shaken in 1947 by the missionaries' willingness to fling themselves into institutional programs. The missionaries were profoundly shaken also by that 1947 deputation. Two of the most highly respected bishops in Lancaster Conference, Amos S. Horst and J. Paul Graybill, accompanied Orie on that trip. And in their portfolios they carried a mimeographed draft of a *Foreign Missions Polity* for acceptance by the missionaries.

These three deputies had stopped briefly in Cairo, Egypt, before flying south to Tanganyika. Before retiring for the night in one of Egypt's fine hotels, one of the bishops pulled the polity from his case and handed it to Orie. "Read this tonight," he requested, "and tell me in the morning what you think of it."

At dawn when Orie returned the booklet the bishop asked, "How does it strike you?"

Orie's response was typically to the point. "It's well done, but the missionaries won't like it."

And they didn't. The missionaries responded that they could not in conscience accept the polity because, in their opinion, it undercut the freedom of the African fellowship.

The reaction of the missionaries deeply disturbed the deputation bishops. One morning at the mission's Bukiroba station Orie found Amos Horst standing forlornly in front of the bungalow where he was staying. Bishop Horst acknowledged Orie's presence and asked simply, "Now what?"

Orie responded, "You have three choices. Either send them all home and start over again, or ask them to write their own polity, or accept their suggestions and rewrite your polity."

The two bishops decided on the latter course. They surveyed the attitudes of the missionaries, put the polity back into their satchels, and plunged into a dizzy round of *ugali* meals with African brothers from one end of Musoma District to the other. They enjoyed the fellowship.

When the deputies arrived home, they had to tell their constituency that they had failed dismally in selling the proposed polity to the missionaries. A public meeting was scheduled at East Chestnut Street Church in the heart of Lancaster City. Shortly before the meeting one of the bishops drove to Orie Miller's home in Akron and confessed that he simply could not report what had happened. But Orie gently urged him to tell everything, to hide nothing at all.

The church was filled with more than 500 people when bishops Horst and Graybill took the floor. Solemnly they explained that the missionaries did not believe that Lancaster Conference traditions were applicable to the Tanganyika church. The audience sat in stunned silence as the bishops spoke, and when the report was finished a deep sigh swept the group. Every heart seemed to cry out, "And has it come to this?" But miraculously no one in that disappointed audience suggested that the plunge into mission had been a mistake. The brotherhood sensed that their anguish was the necessary consequence of obedience.

For the next two years the bishops mulled over possible alternatives. Finally in 1949 the scales tipped in favor of the conservatives, and the *Foreign Mission's Polity,* with minimal modifications, was adopted as the regulation for the Eastern Board program. The missionaries in Tanganyika were grieved and perplexed. How, they wondered, could they reverse the indigenous self-governing processes which were already so well under way? How could they be untrue to their consciences where conviction diverged from polity specifics? Sensing their deep frustration an Eastern Board executive advised, "Put the polity in your files, and keep on working." That is what they did. However, in America the polity wasn't in the files; it was on the desk tops.

What were the issues?

First, the polity implied that the Mennonite Church, and especially the Lancaster Conference, was the unique possessor of the whole gospel. The missionaries believed this was arrogant, that it closed the door to learning from others, and that it was an embarrassment to share such a statement with others.

Second, the polity did not approve of communing with Christians of other groups. In Africa Christians of all denominations worked together in close cooperation. So they objected to a fixed rule on the "close" communion issue.

Third, they objected to the bishop-minister-deacon pattern for Africa and the polity statement that the lot should be normative in deciding whom to ordain. They did not want to introduce the lot into African culture where it would suggest magic. They did not want a three-office ministry because of the power mystique which the highest office so often acquires.

That is a sample of the nature of the objections; one could add many others. One problem towered above all others — the idea that the foreign church was to be subsidiary to the Lancaster Mennonite Conference until such a time as the home church decided to grant independence. From the beginning the missionaries had told the Africans that they were an independent church free to decide church policy. "We can't, we dare not reverse the process," they implored.

On the next deputation visit frustration over tangential viewpoints became so acute that Deputy Amos Horst broke into tears. "I understand how you feel," he assured the missionaries, "but at home there is a brotherhood too, and many don't understand. The only way is for us to keep talking and praying."

In order to encourage the missionaries to cooperate, a doctrinal examination was administered to all prospective and furloughed missionaries. Those with divergent viewpoints could be detained in the homeland. By the early 1950s the doctrinal examination had become one of the most difficult events in the missionaries' experience. A paramount concern in the mind of most missionaries was how to be candid, and yet not flunk. Doctrinal questions covered a wide range of issues such as mode of baptism, the lot for choosing the ministry, nonsalaried ministry, life insurance, and distinctive garb. For some missionaries these were non-issues, but to argue the point could lead to embarrassingly long furloughs.

During his 1948 leave Elam Stauffer was in a happy mood. After a year as a widower he had become engaged to schoolteacher Grace Metzler in Tanganyika, and he was eager to get back to Africa to marry her. The buoyant Elam donned a brown plain suit and shoes to match, instead of the traditional black. The sight of a bishop in brown caused ripples of concern in some congregations.

Four years later Elam and his new family returned to the States for another round of furlough, and the consternation of 1948 deepened into dismay. Elam, who had gone to Tanganyika twenty years before as one who ideally embodied the concerns of the most conservative wing of American Mennonitism, shocked a congregation by declaring that he would rather see a church as variegated as a flower garden, than uniform and spiritually dead.

At furlough's end in 1953, the Stauffer family was detained at home until accumulated misunderstandings could be cleared up. Other missionaries were given ex-

The Elam Stauffers relax outside their tent at the annual missionary conference about 1949.

tended furloughs too. The atmosphere crackled with apprehension. At the height of the crisis Elam met with some friends in Goshen College, Indiana, who pried rather extensively into the reasons for his detention in the United States. At the close of the conversation Professor Paul Miller advised, "I have learned that it is never wise to lock horns with those with whom I disagree. You must find a way to work together." That was tough advice, but Elam followed it, and within six months returned to Africa with his family.

Slowly and painfully a constitution was written for the Tanganyika church. The field church wrote it with guidance from America, but the final document was revised and approved by home church officers. The crisis year was 1959. The Lancaster Conference bishops wrestled within their souls on the nature of the constitution, and whether they were now ready to substitute fraternalism for paternalism. Some backed off from such a far-reaching decision. Powerful voices urged perpetual paternalism. Others wanted a clause demanding approval from the home church before any amendments could be made to the constitution. In the meantime, in Tanganyika national independence was only a year away. Missionaries warned that the African brotherhood could not accept continued control from America. The hour was already late. The church must be given full and complete autonomy.

During this crisis a deputation went to Tanganyika to participate in the twenty-fifth anniversary celebrations of the beginning of the Mennonite Church there. In an outpouring of love and fellowship missionaries, deputies, and Africans shared together the joys of what God was doing. The deputation was grateful, though, that all missionary men still wore the plain coat.

But scarcely had the ink dried on those first triumphant letters home, than the deputies were rudely jolted. This time it was the Ethiopian missionaries, not the Tanganyikans, who rocked the boat. When the deputies arrived in Ethiopia, most of the missionary men showed up at the airport in business suits and ties. It was a difficult moment! The mood of the home church leadership was one of no nonsense. There was no certainty that the bishops would accept autonomy for the Tanganyika Church. Several missionaries were being delayed at home because of the usual doctrinal tangles, and there were strong voices urging that enough was enough. Some were prepared to prevent any and all missionaries from returning to the field who did not fully fit into the doctrinal and disciplinary mold of Lancaster Conference.

Late in the summer of 1959 a group of missionary children were playing hide-and-seek on Bishop Christ Lehman's lawn along Blue Rock Road west of Lancaster. Suddenly one of the youngsters piped up, "Do you all know what! It seems things just get badder and badder, and then they get worser!" And indeed the children seemed to be right!

Miraculously, however, the Lord came near and within the next twelve months the impasse was resolved with peace and fraternity. The Lord used Ira Buckwalter, treasurer of Eastern Board, in a special way during those days and months of crisis. He had been one of the deputies to Africa that year. At strategic moments he would affirm, "I believe that what I saw in Tanganyika is the work of the Holy Spirit. We must not, we dare not block it in any way." Orie Miller reminded the American brethren that the Jerusalem church some nineteen centuries earlier had renounced Jewish paternalism over Gentile churches. He urged that Lancaster Conference learn from the Spirit who guided that memorable Jerusalem Conference in

Acts.[1] By year's end a satisfactory constitution was approved, and there have been no further missionary detentions.

True to the spirit and the letter of the mission's polity, a deputation arrived in Tanganyika and on August 25, 1960, performed the rites of independence. The General Church Council of the Tanganyika Mennonite Church accepted the constitution, and thereupon the American deputies conferred upon the church the full rights, privileges, and duties of autonomy. "You are now a church," intoned Mission Board Secretary, Paul Kraybill. Perhaps overenthusiastically he added, "We should dig a hole and bury the mission in it forever."

It was a solemn moment, but there was also a certain irony about the whole exercise, for in effect Elam Stauffer had already assured the first little group of baptized Christians at Shirati in 1935 that they were then the church. Indeed, in spite of administrative politics, the African church had been functioning for twenty-five years with maturity and considerable autonomy.

Interestingly, looking back it appears that the African Mennonites have always been more free to determine their church profile than many other denominational groups. Some missions literally attempted to transplant Western style churches into Africa. Hundreds of church congregations across Africa are almost exact replicas of Canterbury, Saint Peters, or Oak Lane both in general architecture and worship formats. Mennonite Church life seems to have been far more fluid.

Perhaps that is the reason the Mennonites have not been plagued by the schismatic independence movements which frequently spin off from denominations with Western rootage. Throughout Africa during the last several decades there has been a profuse multiplication of independent churches seeking to develop a more biblical and/or African Christianity than is normally found in Western transplants. But to date no independence movement has spawned within the Mennonite brotherhood. In fact most Tanzanian Anabaptists are stubbornly loyal to their *Kanisa la Mennonite Tanzania* (Mennonite Church of Tanzania).

In retrospect it seems that a principal function of the church administrators was to stand between the people and the policies. They took the blows. They absorbed the intrigues of politics and the hassles over nothing so that the church could mature in Christ.

The missionaries stood between their African brethren and a frustrated bishop board. Africans never had to bear the brunt of the battle. The missionaries personally absorbed attempts to squeeze the African brotherhood into the mold of an alien expression of faith. The missionaries jealously and passionately guarded the right of the African brotherhood to the freedom and autonomy in Christ which the missionaries believed to be right.

Likewise, there is something Christlike in bishop board minutes that read, "A matter of great importance concerning Africa was discussed." The bishops stood in the breach. They absorbed the frustrations of the missionaries so as to protect the home brotherhood from unsettling disputes and the divisiveness of tangential viewpoints. They were the vital link between the African brotherhood and a concerned constituency at home.

Significantly, brotherhood survived and continued to be experienced throughout the struggle. That is the true beauty of this story!

---

1. Acts 15:1-35.

8. THE BROKEN STOOL
(Changing)

Elam Stauffer couldn't believe his ears! Orie Miller, the prominent defender of indigenous missiology, was telling the leaders of the Tanganyikan church that as far as he was concerned they could bury the rigid ideology of indigenousness, and the sooner the better!

Elam was disturbed. For twenty-four long years the missionaries had been preaching and arguing the virtues of the indigenous church, and now at Mugango station on July 3, 1958, Orie Miller was saying, "Forget it." Elam was a man of deep conviction and he wasn't happy to have his indigenous principles treated so carelessly. He took a long look out the nearest arched window of the drab, thatch-roofed, mud-brick meetinghouse where he and perhaps a dozen church officers were assembled. He stared past nearby shady ironwood trees which hardly concealed an attractive missionary residence Phebe Yoder had recently designed. His gaze rested on the waters of Lake Victoria's Mugango Bay a mile away. He must have felt like going fishing.

Indigenous church growth ideals had grown out of the frustrations of nineteenth-century missions. Too often church development in that earlier era had been fueled by mission bounty. People became Christian for "rice." Furthermore, believers were encouraged to migrate from pagan environs into the safe enclave of the mission compound. This strategy might have effectively insulated the believing community from the allures of certain sins, but it also stimulated artificial faith and curtailed meaningful interaction

107

and witness within the pagan community. Consequently, throughout Asia and Africa the church became ensnared by the compound mentality. The church was a distinctly alien institution. It was not taking root.

To break out of these nineteenth-century trappings, the sages of early twentieth-century missiology developed the indigenous strategy. The word *indigenous* means local. The church had to stand on its own feet in the local setting. A healthy church was like an African stool, it had three legs. The legs were self-government, self-support, and self-propagation. If one denied the church any of those legs, it would topple over. The Mennonite missionaries believed in the indigenous ideals. In fact, for them there was no other practical or scriptural approach.

But in 1958 Orie Miller smashed the stool. He informed the missionaries and the Africans that their indigenous guidelines were in shambles, and that a new perspective he called *partnership* had to emerge. It was not just the Mennonites who witnessed the shattering of their indigenous model. Already in the 1940s leading churchmen were nudging the word *indigenous* aside and slipping the word *partnership* into its place. By mid-century mission administrators everywhere were trying to rethink strategy in partnership terms. And that included the Mennonites.

The last chapter reviewed the tug of war between the African and American brotherhood about the self-governing leg of the indigenous stool. The hassle over that leg made the stool a bit wobbly at times, but it never fell over. Ironically, the real blow to the indigenous stool came from Tanganyika itself when missionaries began suggesting that a trickle of funds into the African church would be a good thing. That astonishing recommendation came from Field Secretary John Leatherman in correspondence dated May 9,

1953. Within months a gentle flow of cash did begin. The self-supporting leg soon fractured, and in 1958 Orie Miller was compelled to intone the death rites for the indigenous strategy.

Why had the missionaries changed their minds?

John Leatherman's letter stated clearly that the fellowship of Calvary demands not only spiritual sharing, but also sharing of responsibilities and wealth. This conviction sprang out of the revival fellowship. Interestingly, the only large mission group in East Africa which has delayed in accepting the partnership model is also the only group that officially resisted the revival. In fellowship with African brothers, the Mennonite missionaries had come to see life a little more through African eyes, and when that happened missionary stiffness in all relationships, including money matters, gradually softened.

That was a revolution! For twenty years missionaries had pursed their lips with "no comment" finality whenever Africans asked what their salary was. No mission financial records were ever shared with Africans. No American money ever went directly or indirectly into Tanganyika church treasuries. Leaders' wages, construction of church buildings, songbooks and supplies — everything relating directly to the African church had to be paid by the local church. Institutions such as the Bible school or hospitals did get funds from America, but not the church.

Africans were tempted to suspect the missionaries. Perhaps funds intended for the African church were being diverted into other projects. If church was the focus of mission enterprise, why was the mud-brick church building the most drab, old-fashioned structure on each station compound? Why couldn't the churches have concrete floors so the sand chiggers wouldn't bite worshipers on Sunday mornings? Why were American funds available for compound workers or anyone employed for missionary or institutional benefit, but not for church workers? Church leaders were the most underpaid persons in the entire mission program.

These undercurrents stimulated the Leatherman letter of 1953. The home board responded cautiously. In 1954 a plan was created so that designated gifts from the American brotherhood could flow directly to the African church without becoming an official part of the mission budget. But even that minimal concession drew complex letters from Orie Miller's Akron office. He warned that this money could imperil the indigenous church. He suggested that a better approach might be to retrench the educational and medical programs to portray clearly that the church was indeed first in priority.

Later in 1954 Orie Miller visited Tanganyika. He had a real treat on that trip. He met with responsible African leadership for the first time. The Africans told him plenty! Suffice it to say that in 1955, with Orie Miller's blessing, the Eastern Board began to budget regularly for African church assistance. For the next five years about $1,500 was contributed annually. The first year that the autonomous Tanganyika church made out its own budget was 1961, and church assistance was then increased to $5,000. Within several more years about $20,000 was flowing into that account annually.

The decision to share funds with the African church was done in a spirit of Christian brotherhood. Although Africans could have permitted missionary policy to poison relations, positive communication continued. In 1953 the mission for the first time opened all accounts for review by Africans, and in 1954 Tanganyikans helped to make out the budget. The Africans were astonished at how little the missionaries received in allowances, and promptly wrote requesting the mission board to treat the missionaries better! They marveled at the astronomical costs of mission operations. In 1953 a good average wage for an unskilled African was about $5 per month. Comparing that with an annual Tanganyika Mission budget exceeding $40,000 was overwhelming. Although that represented only about $3.00 per member for Lancaster Conference, the African brethren thanked the Americans for what they felt to be unbounded generosity.

Accompanying Orie Miller on his 1958 visit to Tanganyika were several bishops and his newly-elected successor, Paul Kraybill. On July 3 the deputies had the first official contact with the executive committee of the Tanganyika church. As noted before, the meeting was held at Mugango station. It was in that meeting that Orie Miller dropped the explosive word that from that day on the goal would be partnership. The missionaries were distressed and some were angered that he had not consulted with them more carefully before dropping that idea into the meeting. Orie's pronouncement was the death knell to the indigenous strategy which the missionaries had pursued with such ardor throughout the years. By announcing that mission and church executive committees should be merged, Orie effectively undercut any possibility of salvaging their indigenous guidelines. There could be no debating the pros and cons of the plan, for Orie had announced a fiat.

African executives in that meeting pried Orie with questions and he answered them well. Ghana had just acquired independence. Tanganyika would be independent soon. Thus, Africans had to take leadership. Africans would need to define what kind of assistance they wanted from the American brotherhood, and the

The first Mennonite church building in Tanganyika.

Mennonites would try to help along as best they could. Within two years the executive committee of the Tanganyika church would carry full responsibility for matters currently handled by the mission. The mission would be swallowed up by the church. The church would decide which missionaries it wanted and which it did not need. Properties would be turned over to the church. Orie went on and on.

Fifteen years later, Orie still chuckled as he remembered the hornet's nest he faced later as missionaries confronted him.

"Soon they'll be living in our houses," they warned.

"That's right," Miller replied.

"And then they'll want the cars, and we will have to walk."

"That's right," Miller replied.

"They might ask some missionaries to leave."

"That's right," Miller replied calmly.

The missionaries were right! Several years later

A Mennonite church at the bishop ordination in 1967.

the home office received a cable from the Tanganyika church requesting prompt recall of two missionary families to the States, and immediate recruitment of better missionaries. The Board replied that the Tanganyikans should send the missionaries home, but "better ones" were not available. So the Tanganyikans graciously patched up the problem on the spot, and kept their missionaries.

As more local people learned to drive church cars, missionary transportation sometimes shifted to the inefficient Musoma bus service or plain shoe leather. One missionary had the good fortune to receive a pledge for funding a private car if it could then be his. But the Tanganyikans rejected the plan. Their reasoning? Missionaries did not know how to use cars. They didn't willingly loan them to others. Later, however, the plan was accepted, and several missionaries did get private cars.

This new partnership relationship demanded a revolution in missionary psychology. Once in exasperation Elam Stauffer wrote the home office that partnership was not partnership at all. It seemed to him that the missionaries had become the lesser partners in the new relationship.

Even Orie Miller wasn't quite prepared for partnership when in 1962 he took his wife of a year on one of his round-the-world pilgrimages. He stopped in Tanganyika. Paul Kraybill had assumed full overseas responsibilities by then and Orie was with him. So was Board Chairman Raymond Charles. This delegation met with church leaders to hammer out final agreements on partnership relationships. The meeting was held at the Bumangi Middle School, a beautiful spot astride inland hills which overlooked the Serengeti Plains.

All went quite well until point four of the agenda. Point four stated that a missionary would be appointed to represent missionary interests to the home church and to inform the American brotherhood about the African fellowship. Point four blew the lid off. It seemed to the Africans that they had been double-crossed. Had not the mission board promised that the mission would be buried forever? Now they were retreating to some form of mission tutelage. Obviously the white brethren were not trustworthy. What kind of information did these whites want to send to their American friends? Had the missionaries become spies of some sort? The invective was so cutting that Orie's wife, Elta, left the school building in frustration to sit in a nearby car, where she tried to regain her equilibrium. To some it seemed that partnership would never survive this terrific battering.

Finally, Orie arose and signaled for quiet. He spoke with firmness, declaring again and again that much of what they were saying about the missionaires was

114

not true. "It's just not true, it's just not true," he insisted, and then breaking into sobs he could go on no longer.

Slowly the vice-chairman of the Tanganyika Mennonite Church, Pastor Zedekia Kisare, arose. Kisare had remained silent during the earlier convulsion. Now he addressed the brethren with tact and authority. "Africans are people," he pointed out. "Free people with rights as human beings. The missionaries are people, and they have rights, and they are free, too. Their freedom must be respected." He pointed out that the anger of that meeting had pushed Brother Miller to tears and that his wife had to leave and was still sitting in the car.

With those words, the Holy Spirit moved upon the group and repentance poured forth as everyone begged forgiveness from everyone else. Together they were all kneeling, praying, weeping, and repenting before the Lord. They sent a message to Elta asking her forgiveness too. Then they went on to point five on the agenda.

What is there in the Christian community that binds believers together in this way? How can all kinds of racial and cultural differences vanish in the fellowship of the cross? How beautiful is partnership in Christ!

The Tanganyikans have a song they sing in moments such as this. This is the chorus:

> Glory, glory, Jesus saves me;
> Blessed be His holy name;
> For the cleansing blood has reached me;
> Glory, glory to the Lamb!

During those beginnings in partnership sharing, the first deputation in reverse took place. Two Tanganyikan brethren visited the American churches in 1961.

115

Pastors Zedekia Kisare and Ezekiel Muganda were the deputies. It was a happy day for the church in America. As these men of God from Tanganyika shared their experience of the gospel, many in America discovered that partnership is a two-way street. African brethren often shared truth in a fresh way. For example, they said that the cross life was choosing to take the backseat of the car, and that Calvary was like a low door that makes you flop on your stomach to get through. American Mennonites were blessed as they learned of Christ from these evangels from Africa.

In more recent years the word partnership has begun to slip from Mennonite vocabulary. Now Mennonites speak more and more of brotherhood, community, fellowship. That is good. It seems that the church is moving beyond the techniques of partnership. That word sounds too businesslike. Mennonites are rediscovering the beauty of brotherhood, and surely there is no way to improve on that word.

Brotherhood! Cantonese, Americans, Hondurans, Tanzanians, Ethiopians — in Christ all are brothers. Probably this is the greatest blessing Mennonites have received through their mission involvement. They have discovered brothers all around the world.

9. THE SAFARI GOES ON
(Continuing)

Commencement Day for the Tanganyika Mennonite Church was Thursday, August 25, 1960. As noted previously two bishops and the board secretary had flown 8,000 miles to Shirati's Katuru Hill to participate in the ceremony. Bishop Donald Lauver of Oakland Mills, Pennsylvania, inscribed the event in his diary.

Brother Kraybill explained, "You are now a church. You have freedom to make your decisions. We shall now be giving you property, schools, clinics, hospitals, etc., as your responsibilities." Following Brother Kraybill's explanation there was a great stillness. The Tanganyika brethren arose and with emotion began to express their unworthiness and were humbled by this experience. Here are some of the expressions we heard:

"It is only the love of God that caused you to do this."

"I have great joy in seeing this wonder of all wonders."

"This melts our hearts."

"There is no political power that works like this."

"No one demanded this grant."

"We praise the Lord for this great love."

All the brethren arose and unanimously said, "Asante sana (thank you very much). Glory be to God in the highest," then sat down in silence.

Our eyes became misty as I suddenly realized I was witnessing something very outstanding and I so undeserving. I felt very much humbled. Today I saw the fruits of 27 years of labor in sacrificial service by our missionary brethren and sisters, one of our brethren (Ray Wenger) whom the Lord

117

took home while in service (also Elizabeth Stauffer), thousands of contributions in sacrificial giving from the home church, and countless prayers that ascended to the throne of God in behalf of the church.

And so it was that the Tanganyika Mennonite Church finally acquired official autonomy as a Mennonite conference in its own right. Immediately the church set about legalizing its existence in Tanganyika. Registration procedures were completed on December 6, 1961, just three days before Tanganyika achieved national independence. The Tanganyikan Mennonites were quietly delighted that they had received full legal autonomy just a step ahead of their government.

Autonomy did not, of course, mean that there were no missionaries around. In fact, the bishop and chairman of the new Tanganyika Mennonite Church was missionary Elam Stauffer, and Simeon Hurst served quietly and faithfully as cobishop. Ever since 1947 there had been sporadic efforts to find an African bishop but all attempts had failed. Perhaps this was because of indifference to the need, but more likely because there was no consensus on whom to ordain. But after 1960 the church began searching with greater urgency.

The larger sacramental denominations in Tanzania were quite conservative in bishop ordinations — at least one diocese had over a 100,000 communicants. That pattern compares favorably with African chiefdoms. Obviously the Mennonites would have looked ridiculous ordaining several bishops for a constituency of 2,000. So they decided to ordain one bishop, even though a single bishop church seemed rather strange to those with Anabaptist sensibilities.

Perhaps a dozen tribes were represented in the

Mennonite fellowship. Although each tribe had its own language, Swahili was the *lingua franca* which Bantu tribes everywhere learned easily, because Swahili belongs to the Bantu language family. However, one of the largest tribal memberships in the church was not Bantu, but Nilotic. The Nilotics were relatively new immigrants from the Nile Valley, and they found Bantu Swahili difficult to master. Thus, language and culture differences within the church posed a tricky problem when selecting one bishop to preside over all.

However, after extensive preparation during 1961 and 1962, 120 delegates [1] from all churches convened at Bumangi station to choose their bishop. But the mood was not right. Spiritually perceptive people urged Bishop Elam Stauffer not to permit the selection processes to continue. Unlike previous ordinations, the Holy Spirit was not giving consensus. However, Elam could not stop proceedings. Instead he and others told the Lord about their concern and committed the situation to Him. According to the constitution, seventy-five percent of the votes was needed for bishop selection.

When the votes were cast, the cleavage between the Nilotic and Bantu parties was painfully clear, and voting was about equally divided between the two. When the tally was announced, the pressure cooker exploded. Although some delegates dispersed quietly to their homes, others attempted to make Bishop Stauffer a scapegoat. They called him to the mess hall of the Bumangi Middle School for questioning later that night. Some delegates accused Bishop Stauffer of jeopardizing the possibility of ever acquiring an African bishop. Other suspicions also percolated to the surface.

After listening to all the complaints, Elam took the low road. He accepted the fact that he was an imperfect bishop, and he requested that they forgive him even as God forgives. Then he startled them by declaring, "And whenever you get an African bishop, he will also fail sometimes, and you will need to forgive him too!" And with that simple reminder, the congregation burst into songs of thanksgiving, shook hands all around, apologized, and went home to await the Lord's time to ordain.

But ordination was still four years away. After two years Bishop Stauffer and his capable assistant, Simeon Hurst, came to the end of their many years of work in Tanzania. That was 1964, and the church still could not choose its man. So at Elam and Simeon's recommendation another missionary, Donald Jacobs, was appointed bishop. Jacobs served for two years until the brotherhood finally achieved consensus.

By American standards this process seems unbelievably ponderous. Actually the calling an African bishop in 1966 represented the climax of twenty years of searching for God's answer. For six years the search was intense. But the church did not dare move ahead on this sensitive matter until it achieved consensus. To have done otherwise would have been at best political, and at worst schismatic.

It is no wonder that the ordination of Bishop Zedekia M. Kisare on January 15, 1967, at Bukiroba was a day of joy and celebration throughout the Tanzania Mennonite brotherhood. Bishops David Thomas and Donald Lauver from the United States were there. Even Bishop Elam Stauffer left his American retirement to rejoice in the event.

Secretary Kraybill's diary includes the following entry:

> (The) morning dawned clear and bright on a big day in the life of the Tanganyika Mennonite Church. Just 33 years ago on Saturday, the 14th, Elam Stauffer stepped ashore in Dar es Salaam.

Veteran missionary Elam Stauffer and Bishop Don Jacobs lead the procession of participants and special guests at the ordination of Bishop Zedekia Kisare in 1967.

That was a great day in the life of the church in America and now a third of a century later a great day dawned in the life of the TMC that probably is just as great and significant as was that January 14, 1934. Soon after breakfast trucks and busses began to arrive from the outlying churches. At 8:45 the TMC ordained men, Elam Stauffer, David Thomas, Donald Lauver, Don Jacobs, Hershey Leaman, and I plus a few other visitors gathered at Zedekia Kisare's house. After a word of prayer we formed a procession to walk to the church. The church was crowded and many more folks were standing as we entered and found our reserved seats. Ezekiel Muganda was in charge of the three-hour service. Hershey Leaman was chorister and Don Jacobs interpreter. Choruses from the various TMC schools were in the audience and they sang on several occasions. It was a remarkable display of talent and of involvement by these young folks in the life of the church. Almost all of their songs were made up for the occasion.

Visitors were introduced and a history of Brother Kisare's life was read. Donald Lauver and Elam Stauffer preached and following that David Thomas spoke briefly and then presided at the ordination. David gave the charge in English and Elam Stauffer read it in Swahili while David, Donald, and Elam shared in the laying on of hands. Following that Don Jacobs led in prayer as the brethren knelt with Brother Kisare while the congregation stood. Following the laying on of hands and a greeting, David turned to the ordained brethren and charged them to accept their brother as their leader and then also to the audience and gave a charge to the church to recognize and accept their new bishop.

Following the ordination service the huge crowd gathered in four or five locations for the noon meal. After the noon meal the crowd again quickly dispersed back to their homes by bus and truck because facilities at Bukiroba would not have been sufficient to provide accommodations for the many hundreds who had gathered for this occasion.

All in all the day was a most fitting and appropriate one and all of us were deeply moved by the spirit and attitude with which the church moved through this occasion.

The ordination of a Tanzanian bishop altered the nature of Mennonite mission involvement in Tanzania. As long as the head of the church was an American, the missionaries had considerable influence in establishing priorities. But as of January 15, 1967, that was no longer true. The Tanzanians set their own goals and the missionaries tried to keep pace!

Perhaps Bishop Kisare's biggest headache was finance. As mentioned earlier, regularly budgeted American funds began to trickle into district church treasuries in 1955. When the church became an autonomous conference, the subsidy was about $2,000 per year, but when the church prepared its 1961 budget, $5,000 was listed for church assistance. Most missionaries on the committees fought this large increase, but they were outvoted. Remembering the traditional conservatism of the home office in funding African leaders' wages, the missionaries expected the home folks to protest the new budget. But they didn't! Missionaries were stunned to learn that the package had been rubber stamped by Eastern Board officials.

By the time Kisare was ordained, leadership wage costs had increased to $20,000 yearly. A salaried ministry had become standard. Leadership wages were siphoning funds from other projects such as Bible school. Local giving was not keeping pace with church growth. And most serious of all, church growth had become tied to American funding, meaning that the rate of new ministerial ordinations had become dependent on the rate of American budgetary increase.

When American budget funds finally stopped growing, Tanzanians saw red lights everywhere. Budget took on critical importance when considering ordination requests. Since new churches required new leadership, the budget squeeze directly influenced church expansion goals. Leadership training could jeopardize the system by producing more leaders than the church could support. So Bible school went into eclipse. Add to all these headaches the perennial warning from America that the Eastern Board would begin to cut the Tanzanian budget within a year or so, and it would seem that Bishop Kisare's inherited financial problems would have baffled Solomon himself.

The American brotherhood quietly noted that administrative niceties and dollars don't necessarily make churches grow. But could the Mennonites have done otherwise? Some other groups, notably the Church Mission Missionary Society of the Church of England, did structure a partnership relationship which never permitted permanent funding for local leadership. Interestingly, there are some remote corners in the Tanzania Mennonite fellowship where American largess has not yet penetrated, and generally these churches are thriving quite well. But to decry precedents established in the pre-Kisare era is really a futile exercise. The critical problem facing both the Tanzanian and American brotherhoods now is how to return to a more indigenous model of self-support. And that is not easy.

Vast areas of Tanzania have not been fully evangelized. The Mennonite congregations are concentrated in a small area about the size of Lancaster County, but Tanzania itself is eight times the size of Pennsylvania. The harvest fields in Tanzania are ripe. How can the American fellowship stand beside the Tanzania church in helping her reach beyond the narrow confines of the current church geography to participate in the evangelization of Tanzania as a whole? In cities such as Dar es Salaam and Moshi, missionaries are working with the Tanzanian Mennonites in the urban frontier. But certainly this is only the beginning, because it is God's will for all Tanzanians to be introduced to the gospel in this generation.

In 1969 I spent one day brothering with the Tanzanian Mennonites in church extension. It was an incredible experience, which indicated the kind of mutual sharing that encourages church growth.

During the early 1960s these people and others had moved north along Lake Victoria's eastern hill lands and settled in the Migori area of southern Kenya. In 1968 the Tanzania church asked my parents, Clyde and Alta Shenk, to move to Migori to help gather these little groups into congregations. In April 1969 my family and I visited Migori, and my father planned a brotherhood happening for me.

124

On brotherhood day we got up before the sun, and loaded the blue Toyota pickup truck with lumber for doors and windows, nails, hammers, and other things useful in building a church. We drove our cargo west into a peninsula which jutted into the lake. It was a thirty- or forty-mile trip. The journey was interspersed with stops, some of them exasperatingly long, for church elders who were to accompany us. Ten miles before our destination the graded road became a track coiling around the maize fields which checkered the bushlands. Time and again as we slipped past remote villages, mothers, children, and even men came running to the roadside waving and clapping, for they knew a church would soon rise in their community. The Pentecostal villages were especially ebullient, but even the "proper" Episcopalians waved heartily.

The "official" track ended about two miles short of the church site at a cluster of grass-roofed houses. As we slowed to a stop, a gray-haired man dressed in a tattered brown soldier overcoat, of World War II vintage, stepped in front of the car and beckoned us to follow him. He turned and ran like a dik-dik up the boulder strewn hill behind the village, zigzagging through the granite rocks and bushes that peppered the hillside greenery. Here and there we drove over charred black spots, evidence that someone had heated granite rocks, which blocked the path, until the rocks had fissured under the combined pressure of fire and hammer. The old man running ahead of us was Nicodemus, the engineer who had made the road.

When we got to the church site, a children's choir met us with a song composed especially for the occasion — a song about working together to build the house of God. Within a few minutes we were all at work. My father set about marking out the foundations. I slid behind the Toyota steering wheel, and a work

125

gang jumped onto the back of the truck. We wound slowly down the road Nicodemus had built, and then circled right, toward the western tip of the peninsula where the lake waters had deposited fine sand suitable for cementing. We parked at the shoreline, quickly loaded the truck with a ton of sand, and then drove the tortuous trail back to the church site. We worked hard. When we finished by late afternoon ten tons of sand lay in a mount next to the foundation markings.

At midafternoon we stopped working, and ate together. The menu was good: *ugali*, chicken, broth, bananas, and tea. The choir sang again.

Later came stone counting time. The congregation had decided that the walls of their church should be stone. People were seeing who could gather the most stones for the project. I wiped a tear from my eye when I saw a mother, surrounded by half a dozen little youngsters with another one obviously on the way, standing beside the second largest pile of stones. Smiling "engineer" Nicodemus stood beside the biggest heap. The church elders congratulated them on their hard work, but reminded them that the job had only begun. By then the sun was dipping toward the lake's western horizon, so we shook *kwa heri* all around, and turned the Toyota toward home.

The memory of that little congregation continues to grip me. Their leaders were not receiving support from America, yet they had joined hands to build a church with their own blisters and sweat. A quarterly visit by their pastor gave them just the encouragement they needed to carry on. Gifts from the American brotherhood [2] in the form of cement, lumber, nails, and aluminum sheeting, which they could not purchase themselves, helped their dream become reality. That is the essence of constructive partnership — helping kingdom dreams come true. Similiar acts of mutual sharing must go on, because brotherhood is forever.

Today the church faces new frontiers. The Tanzanian government is structuring a socialist state that places the development of her people ahead of mere economic advance. The school systems and medical facilities which churches helped to create are becoming public institutions with diminishing church control. The church must learn servanthood as institutions which she once controlled become instruments in the hand of government. The church faces the implications of nonresistance in a military state.

The constitution of the Mennonite Church of Tanzania states that its closest affiliation is with the Mennonites of America. Most denominations in Africa are like that; their closest ties are with fraternal churches thousands of miles away. Yet increasingly all these denominations are reaching out to each other to explore together Christian brotherhood in African settings. The Mennonites are discovering in new ways that their closest geographical brothers are the Pentecostals, Anglicans, Lutherans, and the African Inland Churches, and they are developing deeper ties of fellowship locally. They are also reaching for fellowship with the thousands of other Mennonites, their spiritual cousins, who live in at least a dozen African countries as, for example, the Brethren in Christ Church of Zambia and Rhodesia.

For American Mennonites, mission has been a growing experience. Several times during the travail of mission they have seen that they were wrong. They learned the blessing of repentance. They learned to change their minds under the urging of the Holy Spirit. Even the hallowed edifice of their indigenous patterns could die without undue trauma when a change of course seemed right.

Mission is always commencement; it is the never-

A Tanzanian woman shares her testimony in a Sunday morning worship service in the Bukiroba District.

ending drama of new beginnings, until Jesus comes. Mission is like the widow's oil and flour — the more one shares, the richer in Christ one becomes. American Mennonites gave 2 3/4 million dollars for mission in Tanzania from 1933 to 1973. A Mennonite farmer confides that the wealth he has poured into mission would buy several farms. He is a poor man, but he is an incredibly happy man. Over a hundred missionaries have served in Tanzania. They have come from scores of homes and congregations across North America and even Europe. Three adults[3] and four children died while serving in Tanzania. Parents have given their children, and children their parents; husbands have lost their wives, and a wife her husband. Congregations have sent their leaders and their talents. But the more they have given, the more they have been blessed. And the story goes on.

As the story continues to unfold, there are new frontiers to explore. Mennonites in Vietnam have confronted the tragedy of human nature gone rampant. In Central America ripened fields beg for harvesting.

In Hong Kong missionaries wait expectantly for whatever can be learned from developments in China. In the Philippines and Swaziland missionaries are trying to help indigenous fires spread without smothering them with American presence. In Europe there are cooperative projects with local Mennonites. In Ethiopia revival fire sweeps slowly across the country, and it has not passed the Mennonites by. In Sudan there is opportunity to help war-weary people reestablish their homes and churches.

But most important, Lancaster Mennonites are discovering mission at home. Whether in urban ghettos or the suburban recluses of the wealthy, they are working side by side with other Christians, sharing the good news with spiritually famished Americans.

What are the Lancaster area Mennonites discovering through their safari in mission? That is a question none can fully answer, but it seems that they are learning to trust the Holy Spirit, the Bible, and each other more, and are becoming less afraid to follow Christ. This brotherhood has seen God working, and so they are more confident in the power of the Holy Spirit. They used to theorize that the gospel of Jesus Christ is for all people. Now they know it is true, for their brethren encircle the' globe.

---

1. The church selected 120 delegates because the Book of Acts records that 120 people were in the upper room at Pentecost when the Holy Spirit first baptized the church.

2. Funds to help build this church were contributed by expatriate Mennonite teachers in Kenya who were serving under the Mennonite Central Committee's Teachers Abroad Program (TAP).

3. The deaths of Ray Wenger (1945) and Elizabeth Stauffer (1947) have been noted. In 1969 Alta Shenk, the author's mother, died in an air crash in Kenya. She was buried in the little cemetery on Katuru Hill together with the four missionary children.

A Postscript from Tanzania

Truly God did a great thing when in 1934 He moved the Lancaster Conference to send missionaries to Africa. In that first step you sent only four and the amount of money you budgeted that year was not very much. But there were many prayers and great faith was born in your hearts. To the world what you began to do was small, but in that small thing God was purposing to do a great thing both for you and for us. What began in 1934 is still growing today. You now have several hundred missionaries serving in eighteen countries with mission contributions over 1 1/2 million dollars per year. But of more importance than the number of missionaries and the amount of your giving is the great work which God is doing through your continued obedience to the 1934 vision.

God used you to bring us the gospel of salvation through Jesus Christ. The missionaries you sent were evangelists first and foremost, and for this we thank God. They also had skills of administration, building, mechanics, office work, medicine, and education but they were primarily evangelists. Since the early years, medicine has been used as an evangelistic tool. Today with one large hospital and five clinics this is still so. Missionary involvement in secular schools came largely after World War II and for a time this was a tremendous door for evangelism. Thousands of schoolchildren confessed Christ and joined the church. The schools have now been nationalized but the government still gives us opportunity to teach Bible in all the schools.

Through their evangelistic witness we have come to recognize the missionaries as servants of God who are basically interested in the growth of the church. We are concerned, however, that in recent years missionaries seem to see themselves as professionals first — doctors, nurses, teachers, secretaries, development experts, etc. — and evangelists second or not at all. We ask that you, as a sending church, do not forget your first love — the salvation of souls and the building of the church of Jesus Christ. Send us missionaries who love Jesus, who are primarily interested in the spread of the gospel.

Brother David Shenk speaks about the revival which helped to make the missionary and the African brothers. It is true that the gospel of Jesus Christ which the missionaries brought teaches that we are all God's children, that in Jesus Christians are brothers whether they are black or white. But this is so often theoretical and not practical. The white man from the West is very different from us and we looked to him as teacher and leader but not as brother. How he looked at us I do not know. But in 1942 Jesus began to teach us that we are brothers and that we can fellowship together as equals. Many times since then our differences have raised walls of misunderstanding and distrust between us. But I praise God that each time He has shown us that we need to repent and forgive, and then we can keep on being true brothers again.

Now our church is independent and the missionaries you send work for us. But it is still the way of repentance and forgiveness which allows us to be brothers even though we are different. In this way the missionaries work in harmony with us and we with them. In this way, too, the Mission Board and the Tanganyika Mennonite Church work together in mutual trust and good will. I praise God for what He began to teach us in 1942 because without this Way we could not have become one body in Christ.

I said above that our church is now independent. I mean that the responsibility for conducting the affairs of church here is no longer your responsibility but ours. However, we are still weak in many areas where you are strong. So by God's grace you continue to enable us to do God's work here. I speak with humility when I say that we have a good name in many parts of East Africa. This praise is out of proportion to our size as a small church.

This praise is because you have enabled us through your gifts. Through the efforts of some of your missionaries we have access even to non-Mennonite funds. One example is the modern hospital facility at Shirati. We receive students into our nursing school from the length and breadth of Tanzania. We have been enabled by you in this work, yet our countrymen look to us as though *we* had brought it about. But in fact our resources are very meager. It is your love which enables us to perform this Christian service.

And so it is in many ways. Ours is the responsibility yet it is you who continue to enable us to do far more than our slight resources would allow if we worked alone. You empower us through your prayers, through sending us dedicated missionaries who love Jesus, and through your gifts of love.

My brothers and sisters in Christ, do not weary of your good work. You are not working for us, even as we do not work for ourselves. But your work and ours is unto God. Through this effort we lay up treasure in heaven, and many other sons are brought into the kingdom and built up in the faith.

Zedekia M. Kisare, Bishop
Mennonite Church of Tanzania
Musoma, Tanzania, March 1973

SIGNIFICANT DATES

1914 The EMBMC was founded.

1915 The Lord called Phebe Yoder to go to Africa.

1933 December, Orie Miller and Elam Stauffer began
their investigatory journey to find a place
for mission in Africa.

1934 February 14, Elam Stauffer and Emil Sywulka
first set foot on Katuru Hill, Shirati.

Midnight, February 22, John and Ruth Mosemann with Elizabeth Stauffer left port for
Africa.

1935 September 15, first baptisms at Shirati.

Congregational church council began to function
at Shirati.

1936 Bukiroba Bible School established.

1938 First deputation from America.

Elam Stauffer ordained bishop.

General Church Council approved by the home
board.

1939 Zephania Migire miraculously lived after being
attacked by a cobra.

1942 Revival began among the Mennonites.

1945 June 9, Ray Wenger died in Tanganyika.

1947 Missionaries and Africans decided to cooperate
with government in educational development.

Musoma Press began to function.

Missionaries expressed serious reservations about
the proposed *Foreign Missions Polity*.

June 25, Elizabeth Stauffer died in Kampala,
Uganda.

1949	The Foreign Missions Polity was enacted.
1950	October 6, first ordinations of African pastors. Ezekiel K. Muganda and Andrea M. Mabeba.
	December 10, Zedekia M. Kisare and Nashon K. Nyambok were also ordained.
1951	First boarding school for boys built.
1954	Began subsidizing support of Tanganyika church leaders.
	Leprosarium opened at Shirati.
1958	Mission and church decided to substitute partnership for indigenous patterns.
1960	Musoma Bookshop opened.
	August 25, the Tanganyika Mennonite Church achieved official autonomy with a constitution of its own.
	4,000 students in Mennonite primary schools and 600 in the Musoma Alliance Secondary School.
1961	The first deputation from Tanganyika visited the American brotherhood.
1963	Mennonite congregation organized in Dar es Salaam.
1967	January 15, Zedekia M. Kisare ordained bishop.
1968	The Tanzania church sent missionaries to southern Kenya.
1969	July 21, Alta Shenk died in a Kenya air crash.
1971	Shirati Hospital rebuilt and modernized with funds donated primarily from the Evangelical Central Agency, West Germany.
1973	215 Mennonite congregations in Tanzania.

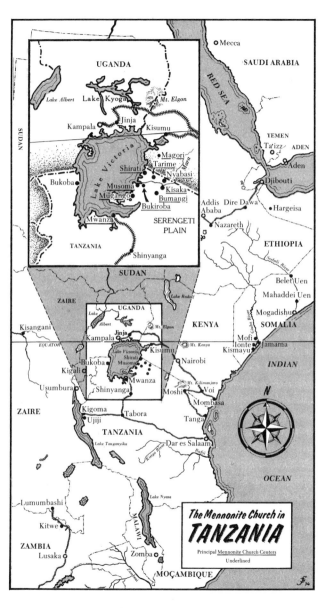

The Mennonite Church in
TANZANIA
Principal Mennonite Church Centers
Underlined

135

THE AUTHOR

David W. Shenk pastors a church in Nairobi, Kenya, and teaches in the Department of Religion at Kenyatta College, University of Nairobi. From 1963-73 Shenk served as a mission leader in Somalia.

He was born in 1937 at Musoma, Tanzania, the son of missionaries J. Clyde and the Late Alta Barge Shenk.

He attended Lancaster Mennonite School, Lancaster, Pennsylvania, received his BA degree from Eastern Mennonite College, Harrisonburg, Virginia, and his MA and PhD degrees from New York University. His dissertation is titled "A Study of Mennonite Presence and Church Development in Somalia from 1950 Through 1970."

He was married to Grace Witmer in 1959. They are the parents of four children: Karen, Doris, Jonathan, and Timothy.

Shenk has authored Christian instruction materials for use among African Muslims, as well as numerous articles on missiology and theological concerns for church-related publications.